Canada's Official Languages:
The Progress of Bilingualism

The coexistence of two official languages in Canada is an emotional and divisive issue. Federal policies encouraging bilingualism are at odds with provincial governments that enact English-only or French-only legislation. The anglophone minority of Quebec and the francophones of other provinces feel increasingly disadvantaged. Richard Joy examines the situation from a statistical perspective, drawing on the results of recent and past censuses to evaluate the changing positions of official-language minorities.

The first part of his book deals with a series of issues including language policies, immigration, and minority-language schools. The second part considers the general questions from a regional perspective, discussing the situation in each region and in the United States.

Joy concludes that official-language minorities are declining in numerical importance in several cases, and in relative importance generally. He recommends that a new question be adopted for the 1996 census if we are to understand precisely the nature of our official-language populations.

Before his retirement in 1985, Richard Joy worked for the Industrial Development Bank and the Department of Regional and Industrial Expansion. He lives in Ottawa.

RICHARD J. JOY

Canada's Official
Languages: The Progress
of Bilingualism

UNIVERSITY OF TORONTO PRESS
Toronto Buffalo London

© University of Toronto Press 1992
Toronto Buffalo London
Printed in Canada

ISBN 0-8020-5007-7 (cloth)
ISBN 0-8020-6938-X (paper)

Printed on acid-free paper

Canadian Cataloguing in Publication Data

Joy, Richard J., 1924–
  Canada's official languages

  Includes index.
  ISBN 0-8020-5007-7 (bound)   ISBN 0-8020-6938-X (pbk.)

  1. Linguistic demography – Canada.   2. Linguistic
  minorities – Canada.   3. Bilingualism – Canada.
  4. Language policy – Canada.   I. Title.

  P40.5.D452C37 1992   306.4'4'0971   C92-093387-4

        23495

This book has been published with the help of a grant from the
Social Science Federation of Canada, using funds provided by the
Social Sciences and Humanities Research Council of Canada.

Contents

Tables

Preface

Two previous studies serve as the foundation for this book. *Languages in Conflict*, written in 1967, cited material available at that time, including data from the 1961 census, and was primarily historical, describing the progress of Canada's two largest language groups during the century following Confederation. In 1978, *Canada's Official-Language Minorities* was published by the C.D. Howe Research Institute as part of its Accent Québec program. Updating the previous study, the work made generally available the basic facts on language use in Canada. The present book builds upon and updates these earlier studies, using census and other data available early in 1991.

Since *Languages in Conflict* was published, several major changes have been made to federal and provincial laws relating to language. In 1969, Parliament declared English and French to be official languages in Canada, a declaration repeated by Bill C-72 of 1988. Also in 1969, New Brunswick became the first (and, to date, the only) province to vote itself bilingual. Both Canada and New Brunswick were formally stated to be bilingual in the Constitution Act, 1982. More recently, Ontario has passed several pieces of legislation that confer a semi-official status on the French language. Meanwhile, however, Quebec, which the Laurendeau-Dunton Commission had held up as a model of bilingualism, declared itself unilingual (French) by legislation passed in 1974 and 1977.

These statutes, and various court decisions, have strengthened the legal status of the French language in Canada, outside as well as inside Quebec. However, these gains were offset by demographics, as the French birth rate dropped to all-time lows and as Quebec had trouble attracting immigrants. From just over 29 per cent of Canada's population in the 1940s, the francophone proportion was down to 24 per cent, measured in terms of the 'home language' criterion of the 1986 census, and there is no indication that the downward trend has not continued.

These events, and their consequences, will be discussed in the following pages. The first part of this book (chapters 1 to 10) deals with such subjects as the census, natural increase, and migration, and the second part with the several regions of Canada. Two appendices present statistical data, both historical and recent.

There is a notable difference between this book and its two predecessors. Rather than merely setting out the historical progress of the two official-language groups, this book is intended to stimulate research into various aspects of Canada's minority-language communities and into the country's official-language policies. Are these policies having the effects desired by their promoters? Are their results commensurate with the effort and money expended on them? In which directions are the various minority communities really heading, including the anglo communities of Quebec?

Regrettably, the language questions asked in the 1986 census, and even those asked in 1991, do not appear to produce the data required for the evaluation of language measures and for the implementation of recent legislation. A completely new question is required, to show the official-language preference of every person in Canada.

In closing, I stress that all opinions presented in this book are those of the author; they do not necessarily have the approval of those friends, members of both official-language groups, who have assisted in the book's formulation.

CANADA'S OFFICIAL LANGUAGES

1

An Overview

On 10 February 1763, Louis XV formally renounced all his claims and pretensions to the former French possessions in North America, east of the Mississippi, with the exception of the archipelago of Saint Pierre and Miquelon. Under the Treaty of Paris, some 80,000 Canadiens and Acadiens became subjects of His Britannic Majesty, completing the transfer of sovereignty begun in 1713 by the Treaty of Utrecht.

Barely twenty years later, the situation had changed drastically. The republicans of what became the United States had achieved their independence, and British North America was reduced to the northern half of the continent, frozen much of the year and only sparsely inhabited. Within this reduced area, the descendants of the French colonists represented a substantial proportion of the entire population and were able to retain their language and their religion.

For almost two centuries after the Treaty of Paris, French remained the preferred language of about 30 per cent of the inhabitants of what is today Canada. It should be emphasized that the use of this language was not confined to Quebec, as there were Acadians in much of the Atlantic region and French-speaking fur traders west of the Ottawa River.

From 1763 on, however, immigrants poured into Canada from the United Kingdom, the United States, and continental Europe. These immigrants, generally, either were English-speaking on arrival or became so after they settled down; only a few of the newcomers reinforced the French-speaking element of the population.

Whenever the rate of net immigration was high, the proportion of French-speakers among Canada's population declined. This trend was reversed during periods of low (or negative) net immigration, as the higher rate of natural increase of the francophones asserted itself. This situation continued throughout the nineteenth century and the first half of the present century. However, by the end of the 1950s, the average size of French-speaking families had begun to shrink. In essence, one factor that had previously favoured the French language has now disappeared.

The 1986 census found that children (aged 0 to 4 years) whose mother tongue was French represented only 23.1 per cent of the total number of Canadian children in that age group. This figure is a new low. It is, also, below the proportion of francophones of all ages in Canada, whether that proportion is measured by the newer census question on home language (24.0 per cent) or by the older 'mother tongue' criterion (25.1 per cent).[1] This finding indicates that the proportion of francophones among Canada's population will continue to decline, even if natural increase were the only factor to consider.

It is true that the birth rate of the French-speaking component of Canada's population has recovered somewhat from a low reached in 1987. However, even after three years of improvement, the rate is still not ahead of that registered by the non-French population.

Meanwhile, other factors must be considered. One of these is language transfer, whereby a person changes from one language to another; despite some gains by the French-speaking community, language transfer has favoured the English language to such an extent that it is virtually synonymous with anglicization.

Attention must also be paid to interprovincial migration. Migratory movement from one province to another does not, of course, directly change the proportions of the various language groups in Canada. However, an infusion of newcomers does maintain the strength and vitality of the minority groups. For this reason, it is significant that recent trends may be quite different from those of a few decades ago: there seems to be a diminishing tendency for French-speakers to move out of the regions in which theirs is the majority language. Meanwhile, the net migration of anglos from Quebec has seriously weakened what was once Canada's healthiest and most powerful minority.

The Laurendeau-Dunton Commission did its work in the mid-1960s, when only migration and anglicization were of recognized

---

1 'Home language' is defined as the language spoken most often by the respondent in his or her own home; 'mother tongue' is the language first learned in childhood and still understood.

significance. Not surprisingly, its report did not emphasize what may be the most important problem facing Canada's French-speaking minority today, that of mere survival in the face of low birth rates. Also, at the time that the commission was preparing its report, it was still possible to inspire genuine sympathy for the French-speaking minorities outside Quebec by pointing to the status of the English language within Quebec.

The situation has changed. The voting power of French Canadians has already declined, a factor that must always be considered by governments. Of more importance, Quebec can no longer be cited as a successful example of bilingualism. The English-speaking majority in Canada is showing a reduced willingness to support an official-languages policy that promotes the use of French in all parts of Canada, but that, rightly or wrongly, is perceived to be indifferent to the decline of the anglo minority in Quebec.

The 1986 census showed a Canada within which the two official languages did not have equal status from coast to coast. In the interior of Quebec, very little English was spoken, and French was the universal language. The south and west of Quebec (Montreal, plus the Eastern Townships and the Gatineau area) and the northern half of New Brunswick were bilingual regions, with French-speaking majorities. Northern and eastern Ontario was another 'region of contact' but differed from the two described previously in that, there, English was unquestionably the predominant language. Everywhere else in Canada, English was the common language, and French-speakers were found only in scattered islands.

Tables 18, 19, and 20, in Appendix A, show the development of the French component of Canada's population over the past century. 'Language spoken at home' has been asked only since 1971, and even 'mother tongue' data are available only from 1931, so table 20 gives data for the number of persons reporting French as their ethnic origin, at the censuses of 1881 to 1971.

From these tables, it can be seen that the proportion of French-speakers among Canada's population peaked in 1941 or 1951 and has, since that time, been trending downwards. From other data in this book, it will be seen that there has been an increasing polarization of Canada's two official-language groups, a polarization frequently cited in support of giving special status to Quebec.

Other tables in Appendix A show the slow rise of official bilingualism in each of several areas of Canada and the number of immigrants living in Canada at each of the various censuses, from 1881 to 1986.

Finally, the tables in Appendix B present language data from the 1986 census, showing 'home language' and 'mother tongue' figures for Canada and for each of several provinces where the minorities are particularly numerous.

2

The Progress of
Official Bilingualism

For better or for worse, a fact of life in Canada is that most of its citizens belong to one or the other of two major language groups. In 1986, English was the language spoken in the home by 69 per cent of the population, French by 24 per cent, and both these languages have official status under federal law.

Canada is, of course, not the only country with more than one official language, and there are many ways of dealing with the practical problems that can arise from such a situation. In Belgium, the solution has been to draw a line between the Flemish-speaking north and the French-speaking south; the two languages coexist within the city of Brussels. In Switzerland, each canton decides its own language policy, and bilingual districts, such as that of Biel/Bienne, are the exception.

Other countries follow quite different policies. The two superpowers were surprisingly similar in this respect. Russian was the universal language of the former Soviet Union, although each constituent republic was free to have its own language taught in the schools. American English is the language used throughout the United States, although frequently Spanish-speakers are provided with services in their own language.

Regardless of these and other practices, the major federal parties in Canada have expressed the view that both the English and the French languages should have official status from coast to coast. To promote this ideal, the Liberals passed the Official Languages Act in 1969; in 1988, the Progressive Conservatives passed a new version that may go farther than the original ('may' because much will depend on the regulations that must be made for implementation of this act).

Official bilingualism was entrenched in the Constitution Act of 1982. Section 16 of the act states that English and French are the official languages of Canada and have equal rights and privileges as to their use in all institutions of the Parliament and the Government of Canada. The same section applies the same equality to all institutions of the legislature and government of New Brunswick, the only province that is, constitutionally, bilingual.

Several other sections also deal with bilingualism, notably sections 17 to 20; section 21 ensures that the English-speaking minority in Quebec and the French-speaking minority in Manitoba will continue to enjoy the limited rights granted by section 133 of the Constitution Act, 1867 (formerly, the British North America Act), and by section 23 of the Manitoba Act, 1870. Section 22 protects any rights or privileges of the non-official languages. Section 23, which sets out the constitutional right of certain citizens to enrol their children in minority-language schools, will be discussed, in detail, in chapter 10.

Language Polarization
At the 1986 census, some six million persons reported French as the language they spoke most often in their own homes (after allocation, by Statistics Canada, of a share of all multiple responses that included 'French'). Of those reporting French as their 'home language,' just over 5.3 million were living in the Province of Quebec and nearly 0.5 million more were in northern New Brunswick and the north and east of Ontario, regions that are adjacent to Quebec.

Thus, less than 4 per cent of Canada's francophones were living in the rest of the country, a vast expanse that includes southern Ontario, the four western provinces, the northern territories, and most of the Atlantic region. Conversely, less than 5 per cent of Canada's English-speaking population was found within the Province of Quebec.

This progressive concentration of Canada's French-speakers within Quebec and adjacent areas of Ontario and New Brunswick prompted the comment: 'If Canada's duality is not in doubt, it is increasingly characterized by polarization.'[1] This trend, which would have been given official recognition by the 'distinct society' clause of the Meech Lake Accord, might well result in a divided country, with Quebec French-speaking and most of the rest of the country equally unilin-

---

1 Commissioner of Official Languages, *Annual Report, 1990* (Ottawa 1991), xiv

gual, but English-speaking. The two languages could coexist only within a narrow bilingual belt; elsewhere, with their present federal support withdrawn, the linguistic minorities would eventually disappear through assimilation or out-migration.[2]

The statistics are worth reciting. Within Quebec, some 3.8 million people told the 1986 census that they spoke only French. Of Quebec's total population of 6.5 million, 94 per cent claimed to be able to carry on a conversation in French, as against only 40 per cent who reported that they could converse in English.

Outside Quebec and northern New Brunswick, the prevalence of the English language is even more remarkable than is that of the French language in Quebec. Throughout the rest of the country, English is the universally understood language and is spoken by more than 98 per cent of the population; many of the remaining 2 per cent are persons who speak neither official language. Even after counting all those for whom French is merely a second or third language, less than 10 per cent of the population claimed to be able to converse in it, in eight provinces and both territories.

It is difficult to insist on French-English bilingualism in Quebec, where 60 per cent of the population cannot carry on a conversation in English and where provincial law (sections 45 and 46 of Bill 101) forbids the requirement of any language other than French as a job qualification, unless the employer can prove that a knowledge of that other language is essential to performance of the work.

It is probably even more difficult to insist on bilingualism in Ontario, where seven persons out of every eight are unable to converse in French. West of the Great Lakes and east of Moncton, it is unrealistic to make bilingualism a requirement for federally influenced employment: almost 99 per cent of the people in this area can speak English, but only 6.5 per cent claimed, in 1986, to be able to carry on a conversation in French.

Efforts by the federal government to increase the general level of official-language bilingualism have, in at least some well-publicized cases, resulted in a backlash against the second language. As one example, both Saskatchewan and Alberta used the alternative offered to them by a Supreme Court decision[3] and, in 1988, passed laws

2 Cf. Richard J. Joy, *Canada's Official-Language Minorities* (Montreal: C.D. Howe Research Institute 1978), 41.
3 *Mercure* v. *A.G. Sask.* [1988] 1 SCR 234

repealing the vestigial rights of French in the respective provincial legislatures.

Meanwhile, encouragement of the use of the English language within Quebec has elicited hostile reactions from politicians at all levels. In December 1988, the provincial government of Robert Bourassa used the 'notwithstanding' clause of the Charter of Rights and Freedoms to pass Bill 178 and, thereby, to deny anglos the right to use their own language on public signs visible from outside their establishments.

The record of the federal government has also been publicly criticized. For example, the federal public service in Quebec employs far fewer anglos than the number corresponding to their proportion of the province's population.[4]

Some of the implications of a continuing polarization of Canada's two official languages can be found in a recent study published by Quebec's Conseil de la langue française. This study suggests that 'la francophonie hors Québec' could become merely a case of the younger generations being aware of their French ancestry but speaking only English (this is a common situation in the United States, where the grandchildren of immigrants from Quebec are often incapable of conversing in French).[5]

With regard to the situation within Quebec, the study states clearly that 'it is probably less costly for a young unilingual Anglophone to move out of Quebec than to acquire an acceptable command of the French language.'[6]

Immersion Courses

Perhaps the most important element in the federal government's policy on promotion of both official languages from coast to coast is the hope that future generations will learn the second language during their younger years and so be able to function in both English and French. This would reflect, of course, the personal situation of Pierre Elliott Trudeau, who was Canada's prime minister in 1969, at the time that the Official Languages Act was passed by Parliament.

School statistics do not support this dream. During the 1988–9

---

4 Commissioner of Official Languages, *Anglophone Participation in the Federal Public Service in Quebec*, report submitted to the Governor in Council (Ottawa 1987)

5 Institut Gamma, *Prospectif de la langue française au Québec*, no. 25 in the series Documentation du Conseil de la langue française (Quebec City 1987), 239

6 Ibid, 57 (my translation)

TABLE 1
Percentage of population fifteen years of age and over, replies to 'official languages spoken,' Canada, censuses of 1971 and 1986

	1971	1986
English only	66.3	66.3
French only	15.6	14.3
Both English and French	16.7	18.3
Neither official language	1.4	1.1

school year, only 227,975 students were enrolled in French-language immersion courses in all of Canada outside Quebec. That figure represents barely more than 6 per cent of the eligible school enrolment of 3.6 million. Of equal importance: only 67,960 of the students in immersion were in Grades 7 to 13, out of a possible total of 1.7 million.[7] To quote from an interview given by Mrs Kathryn Manzer, then president of Canadian Parents for French: 'For most children, immersion terminates at the end of Grade 8 ... They're not going to get jobs at age 20 with a 14-year-old's vocabulary.'[8]

The Census Record

The census of 1971 was taken less than two years after passage of the Official Languages Act. That of 1986 is the most recent for which results have been published. What progress was made, during the intervening fifteen years?

Table 1 shows the census results obtained from the 'official languages spoken' question asked at those two censuses (to minimize the effect of age, this table excludes those persons who were younger than fifteen years as they tend to be predominantly unilingual and made up only 22 per cent of Canada's population in 1986, as against 30 per cent in 1971). As can be seen from this table, 32.6 per cent of the population age fifteen and older claimed to be able to converse in French in 1986, compared to 32.3 per cent in 1971. During the same period, the proportion claiming conversational ability in English rose from 83.0 per cent to 84.6 per cent.

More detailed figures may be found in table 21 of Appendix A:

---

7 All data are from Statistics Canada, *Minority and Second Language Education*, Catalogue no. 81-257 (annual) (Ottawa 1990).
8 Orland French, in the *Globe and Mail*, 7 October 1989, D2

these show that, for the population of all ages, there has been a noticeable upward trend in each section of the country, since at least 1961, with regard to the proportion claiming to be able to converse in both English and French, but that the proportion of bilinguals is still very low, except in Quebec and, to a somewhat lesser extent, in New Brunswick.

The Cost of Official Bilingualism

It is difficult to set a cost for the various measures designed to promote the use of both French and English in Canada. The annual report of the Commissioner of Official Languages lists just over $626 million of expenditures by federal departments and agencies, but this amount would not include the probably much larger sums being spent by the private sector.[9] In this latter regard, it should be noted that federal legislation governing bilingualism is complex; for example, the bilingual labelling of packages is required under the Consumer Packaging and Labelling Act, not under the Official Languages Act.

Some Problems

Reference has been made earlier in this chapter to the reactions noted, both outside and inside Quebec, against federal promotion of French-English bilingualism. The attitude of the Quebec government is that the French language must be protected and that federal attempts to promote the English language are not welcome. Meanwhile, despite legislation in favour of the French language in New Brunswick and Ontario, the attitude of the general population outside Quebec does not seem as supportive of federal measures as it was in 1969.

9 Commissioner of Official Languages, *Annual Report, 1989* (Ottawa 1990), 254

3

The Census of Canada

In any study of demographic and linguistic trends, much of the numerical data come from the responses to census questions. Anyone using such data should be familiar with the strengths and weaknesses of the census material.

On the strength side, it can be stated that Canada makes a special effort to measure the linguistic characteristics of its residents. In 1986, there were three census questions on language plus one each on ethnic origin and place of birth. In 1991, these five questions were again asked, plus a question on religion and a completely new question on non-official languages spoken (the 'religion' question had been asked in 1981 but was omitted in 1986). As the censuses also asked age, sex, place of residence, income, education level, etc., it is possible to make up a broad list of cross-classifications of the data.

However, the weaknesses of the census data are admitted even by Statistics Canada and cannot be ignored. Three useful sources of information on these weaknesses are: cautionary notes found in many census publications; public statements by officers of Statistics Canada; and comments to be found in papers written on census-related subjects.

In its *Census Handbook* (1986 census publication 99–104), Statistics Canada has listed five types of errors that can affect census data. These are:

- coverage errors, which occur when there has been undercount or overcount (the latter is less common);
- non-response errors, which occur when no response has been given to a question;

- response errors, which occur when the question is misunderstood and incorrectly answered;
- processing errors, which occur in the handling of completed questionnaires; and
- sampling errors, which are related to the choice of households to which the long-form questionnaire is sent.

Overcounts occur when a person has been counted more than once or when someone is counted who should not have been (e.g., someone who is in Canada on a temporary visa). *Undercounts* occur when a household member is forgotten by the person filling out the questionnaire or when a building is missed by the person distributing census forms. Recently, there has also been comment on the undercount that can arise from omission of the homeless.

Statistics Canada believes that approximately 2 per cent of Canada's population were missed in 1981 and that, because of budget restrictions, the proportion of undercount may have been 3.2 per cent in 1986 (1991 estimates are not yet available). The proportion varied from one province to another, with Quebec slightly (0.1 per cent) below the national average in the censuses taken in 1981 and 1986. Unfortunately, it is not possible to provide even an estimate of the undercoverage in each census division.[1]

Certain groups are particularly susceptible to undercount, a factor that must be kept in mind when preparing profiles based on census data. There seems to be general agreement that, in the 1986 census, males aged 20–24 were undercounted by more than 10 per cent, while counts of some other groups were probably accurate to within about 1 per cent.[2]

Undercoverage is of particular importance to those who must work with intercensal changes (for example, when estimating the number of persons who have emigrated); the combination of a relatively low undercount in 1981 and a high undercount in 1986 would seriously complicate certain calculations.

Statistics Canada is well aware of the consequences of coverage errors, but remedial action would add to the cost of each census and,

1 Ivan P. Fellegi, 'Le sous-dénombrement dans le recensement canadien,' in *Le Devoir*, 18 January 1982
2 Céline Fortier and Ronald Raby (of Statistics Canada), 'Evaluation de la qualité des données par âge et sexe du recensement de 1986 au niveau national,' in *Cahiers québécois de démographie*, Autumn 1989, 290

in any case, complete accuracy could never be achieved. It should be noted that undercoverage is certainly not confined to Canada; the 1990 census of the United States is believed to have missed 4.8 per cent of all the Blacks in that country and 1.7 per cent of the non-Blacks.[3]

Returning to the Canadian scene, undercounting of a special type occurred in 1986, when the residents of a number of Indian reserves boycotted the census. Fortunately, this boycott affected only 0.2 per cent of Canada's total population; Statistics Canada estimated the number of persons thus missed as being 44,733, including 7,815 in Quebec.

Non-response errors occur when one or more of the census questions are not answered; this happens in 1 or 2 per cent of all cases, despite follow-up procedures used for certain key questions. Statistics Canada imputes answers to such questions but notes that this practice can result in some loss in accuracy.[4] This loss can be particularly serious when the non-respondents differ in some major respects from the respondents, since imputations are based on the replies given by the latter.[5]

Response errors occur when the question is answered incorrectly; the wording of the question may be a factor. For example, in 1971 the heading 'mother tongue/langue maternelle' may have misled some respondents into reporting the usual language of their mothers, rather than the language they themselves had first learned in childhood and still understood.[6] This heading was deleted in subsequent censuses.

Another type of response error was noted in 1986 when 25,520 persons of French mother tongue in Quebec replied 'French only' to the census question on official languages spoken, yet reported English as the language they spoke most often in their own homes.[7] No blame can be attached to the wording of the question in this case.

Processing errors can arise from the human factors involved in pro-

3 Robert A. Mosbacher (U.S. Secretary of Commerce), in *Census*, August 1991, 1–4

4 Statistics Canada, *Census Handbook*, Catalogue no. 99-104E (Ottawa 1988), 86

5 Statistics Canada, *Profile of the Immigrant Population*, Catalogue no. 93-155 (Ottawa 1989), xxxii

6 Association des démographes du Québec, 'Mémoire: Recommendations pour la recensement de 1981,' in *Cahiers québécois de démographie*, June 1975, 52–3

7 Statistics Canada, *Language Retention and Transfer*, Catalogue no. 93-153 (Ottawa 1989), 3–55

cessing the completed census questionnaires.[8] Also, defective printing of forms may cause the computer to produce an erroneous count.[9]

Sampling errors include, in addition to those related to the choice of households that will receive the long questionnaire, aspects related to weighting, i.e., the choice of factors that must be applied to the sample data received.[10]

These sources of error are of particular importance when measuring small minorities. To quote the chief statistician: 'The sampling error becomes serious when one is talking about very small areas.'[11] To support Dr Fellegi's statement, some data from the 1981 census can be cited; both the 2A (100 per cent coverage) and the 2B (sample) figures were published for the 'mother tongue' question of this census.

In the Province of Quebec, a large area, there was a difference of 1.6 per cent between the 2A and 2B figures for the number of persons of English mother tongue.[12] This difference may be attributed chiefly to the sampling procedure, which specifically excluded 'inmates of institutions' from the 2B data, but included them in the 2A data.

However, the difference is far wider when small areas are considered. Because of the presence of a major home for English-speaking old people, census tract 103 of the City of Sillery contained 41 per cent fewer anglos by the 2B measurement than by the 2A method. Even this discrepancy was far exceeded by the 99 per cent difference reported for census tract 315 of the City of Verdun, where almost all the residents were inmates of the Douglas Hospital and, therefore, excluded from the 2B sample.[13]

---

8 Reply to question no. 3102, *Hansard,* 26 November 1975, 9467
9 J.M. Kralt, *Processing and Its Impact on the 1971–1976 Census Mother Tongue Data* (Ottawa: Statistics Canada 1977), 8–9
10 Statistics Canada, *Census Handbook,* Catalogue no. 99-104E (Ottawa 1988), 87
11 Ivan P. Fellegi, *Minutes* of the Joint Committee on Official Languages, 30 October 1989, 3:28
12 Difference obtained by comparing the English mother tongue population of the province as reported for the sample population (694,915) with that reported for the entire population (706,115); these numbers are found in Statistics Canada's 1981 census publications *Census Divisions,* Catalogue nos. 95-942 (sample population) and 95-902 (entire population) (Ottawa 1983 and 1982).
13 Data obtained from statistics Canada's 1981 census publications *Census Tracts Québec,* Catalogue nos. 95-965 (sample population) and 95-924 (entire population) (Ottawa 1983 and 1982) and *Census Tracts Montréal,* Catalogue nos. 95-959 (sample population) and 95-918 (entire population) (Ottawa 1983 and 1982).

The Pitfall of Changing Boundaries

There is always the possibility that a geographical unit may change between censuses. When making historical comparisons, it is essential to ensure that the data compared have come from exactly the same area, or that changes in the geographical area are drawn to the reader's attention.

This comment is applicable to census districts and to municipalities, which sometimes change boundaries between censuses. It is particularly relevant when dealing with census metropolitan areas (CMAs), which tend to expand in accordance with a definition developed by Statistics Canada (for example, the Montreal CMA covered 2,814 km² in 1981 but had expanded to 3,509 km² in 1986).

As an example of the problems that can be caused by this variation in boundaries, students of minority languages were, at first, quite excited by the fact that the proportion of anglos in the Quebec City CMA took an upward jump in 1971, reversing the long-term trend. However, analysis showed that this reversal was entirely attributable to expansion of the CMA to include the municipality of Shannon, in Portneuf County, which brought an additional 1,590 persons of English mother tongue into the CMA.

Even data for all of Canada must be used only with care. A census taken prior to 1949 would not include Newfoundland. One consequence of that is of particular importance to the theme of this book: the decline in the proportional strength of Canada's French population that occurred between 1941 and 1951 can be attributed to the entry into Confederation of a third of a million predominantly English-speaking Newfoundlanders. Within the pre-1949 boundaries of Canada, the proportional strength of the French mother-tongue population actually increased between 1941 and 1951.

Changes Over Time

'Mother tongue' sounds solid and unchanging. So do the names of other census criteria. Unfortunately, most of these criteria did not even exist one hundred years ago, and those that have been in existence for many decades have often been changed to such a degree that comparison over the years is of questionable validity.

Language questions were not included in the censuses of the nineteenth century, and even 'origins of the people' was not introduced until 1871.[14] An early version of the census question on official lan-

14 Census of Canada, 1871, vol. 1, xxii

guages spoken was introduced in 1901, for persons five years of age and over, and a question entitled 'Mother Tongue' (for persons ten years of age and over) appeared on the 1921 questionnaire. However, it was not until 1931 that a question approximating today's 'mother tongue' was addressed to the entire population.

The 1931 version of the 'mother tongue' question asked the 'first language learned in childhood *and still spoken.*' The question was materially changed in 1941, the italicized phrase becoming 'if still understood.'[15] This question has remained substantially in the same form in all subsequent censuses, but editing procedures have varied from one census to another and, in 1991 as in 1986, the instructions that accompanied each questionnaire actually asked that multiple responses (e.g., 'English + French') be given, whether these seemed appropriate. Incidentally, 1986 was the first census for which the number of multiple responses, to the 'home language' as well as to the 'mother tongue' question actually appeared in every publication; in previous censuses, Statistics Canada had reduced multiple responses to a single language through application of editing procedures that varied from one census to another.

'Home language,' the language most often spoken by the respondent in his or her own home, was introduced into the census questionnaire in 1971, after the Laurendeau-Dunton Commission had criticized the 'mother tongue' question for eliciting answers that were 'a generation behind the facts.'[16] This criterion discloses any shift in language that may have occurred during the respondent's lifetime and is not based on the language that he or she spoke (or learned, as the case may be) during childhood.

Unfortunately, the wording of the new question was not quite that recommended by the commission's report, and the question has been criticized (correctly, but probably too severely) as being 'of little significance in that the language spoken at home is often determined by the unilingualism of one of the members of the household' (my translation of 'relativement faible, puisqu'elle est déterminée souvent par l'unilinguisme d'un des membres du groupe ou de la famille').[17]

Even with this flaw, 'home language' may well be the most au-

15 Census of Canada, 1941, vol. 1, 268
16 Royal Commission on Bilingualism and Biculturalism, *Report*, Book 1 (Ottawa 1967), 18
17 D'Iberville Fortier, in *Minutes* of the Joint Committee on Official Languages, 28 November 1989, 5:34

thentic measure of the minorities that can be found in the census. However, it was asked of only a sample of the population in 1991, as in previous censuses. In large measure in keeping with the wording of section 23 of the Charter of Rights and Freedoms, the older question on mother tongue was the only language question asked of the entire population.

Official Bilingualism

The results obtained from the question on official languages spoken are often cited as a measure of official bilingualism. However, in 1987–9, Statistics Canada tested a somewhat differently worded question 'which stipulated the ability to carry on a fairly long conversation on different topics,' and analysis of the results 'revealed a fairly significant decline [une baisse assez importante] in the proportion of bilingual respondents.'[18] In other words, the 1986 census question had tended to inflate the number of respondents classified as being officially bilingual.

None the less, the question asked in 1991 was essentially the same as that of 1986, on the stated grounds that any change would make it impossible to compare the resulting data with data from previous censuses.

Multiple Responses to the Language Questions

Prior to 1981, all multiple responses (e.g., 'English + French') to the 'ethnic origin' or 'language' questions had been reduced by Statistics Canada to a single response. In 1981, however, multiple responses to the 'ethnic origin' question were not only accepted, but retained for tabulation purposes. At the 1986 census, this change was extended to the 'home language' and 'mother tongue' questions. Also, as has been noted earlier in this chapter, multiple responses to the language questions were not only accepted, but actually invited.

Speaking to the Joint Committee on Official Languages on 31 October 1989, Canada's chief statistician deplored the fact that the high levels of multiple responses to the 'mother tongue' question (955,000 in 1986) and to the 'home language' question (1,160,000) made analysis of the census data 'more complex.' To quote Dr Fellegi: 'How should one estimate the size of a language group? Should the multiple responses be added to the group of respondents reporting the lan-

18 Ivan P. Fellegi, in ibid, 31 October 1989, 3:7

guage in question?'[19] Various aspects of this problem are discussed in the next chapter.

Recognizing this concern, Statistics Canada had published *Adjusted Language Data* in April 1988. In this report, the multiple responses of 1986 were distributed in accordance with formulas developed from the 1981 census. However, those using adjusted language data must keep in mind that, despite the mathematics, the distribution was merely a best guess as to the intentions of those who returned multiple responses to the two language questions of the 1986 census.

Statistics Canada subsequently published *Population Estimates by First Official Language Spoken*. This report will be discussed in the next chapter, since it was intended to quantify the various linguistic minorities while working from the available census data.

In the long questionnaire used in 1991, the four questions related to language were grouped together, in the expectation that doing so would considerably reduce the incidence of multiple responses.[20] Whether the hoped-for degree of reduction will be achieved is still not known, but it must be kept in mind that 80 per cent of the multiple responses received in 1986 to the 'mother tongue' question came from persons returning the short questionnaire, on which there was only one language question.

Need for a Continuing Body

It has been suggested that an important job of the U.S. Census Bureau is to 'provide statistics for national purposes ... many of the decade's new laws, executive orders and agencies require more extensive and detailed data about minorities than had previously been produced by the statistical system.'[21] This comment appears to be equally applicable to Canada, where a completely new census question appears required, as described in the last section of the next chapter.

The Second Bilingual Districts Advisory Board expressed its 'surprise' at discovering that there was no continuing body responsible for collecting information on Canada's language populations.[22] However, the government turned down the board's recommendation that

19 Ibid, 3:5
20 Ibid, 28 November 1989, 5:5
21 Harvey M. Choldin, 'Statistics and Politics: The "Hispanic Issue" in the 1980 Census,' in *Demography*, August 1986, 415
22 Second Bilingual Districts Advisory Board, *Report* (Ottawa 1975), paras. 1164–74

such a body be created.[23] Had this recommendation been accepted, the body would have been able to advise Statistics Canada on the information required at each census, to ensure that the data would meet the needs of current government policies on linguistic minorities.

It is true that proposals for the 1991 census were examined and discussed by the Standing Joint Committee on Official Languages. Unfortunately, the MPs and senators who sit on this committee have many other matters requiring their attention and they cannot be expected to give their time fully to language matters.

23 Honourable C.M. Drury (acting president of the Treasury Board), in *Hansard*, 21 November 1975, 9328

4

Who Is an Anglo
(a Francophone)?

The preceding chapter described the census of Canada and pointed out that, despite its several strong features, this census also has some weak points. Unfortunately for those who must use the census to identify Canada's linguistic-minority communities, the weaknesses of the census are most evident when the populations to be examined are small.

In other words, if the census states that approximately one-quarter of Canada's 1986 population was of French mother tongue, then this statement can be accepted as being reasonably exact. However, for many small municipalities the data published by Statistics Canada are of only 'limited reliability,' even if the information was collected on a 100 per cent basis.[1]

Incidentally, it should be noted that, although the 'mother tongue' question appeared on the 2A questionnaire and was asked of every member of the population, the response figures used in *Population Estimates by First Official Language Spoken* were those obtained from only the 2B questionnaire, addressed to only a sample of the population and excluding inmates of institutions; this practice introduces additional sources of error.[2]

The Census Criteria
In Canada, the sizes of minorities are usually measured by some variant of either home language or mother tongue. However, these

1 Statistics Canada, *User's Guide to the Quality of 1986 Census Data Sampling and Weighting*, Catalogue no. 99-136E (Ottawa 1990), 43
2 Statistics Canada, *Population Estimates by First Official Language Spoken*, Reference no. 47013 (Ottawa, September 1989), iii

two census questions leave unresolved the problem of what to do with those persons who give a multiple response ('English + French') or a response involving a non-official language.

To some extent, this problem can be resolved by use of the census question on official languages spoken; obviously, someone who can speak only one of the two official languages will not wish to be offered services in the other language. However, the question cannot be used by itself as a measure of the level of government services required in the minority language: at the 1986 census, 2,595,810 persons in Quebec claimed that they could converse in English, while 1,689,340 outside Quebec and New Brunswick claimed to be able to converse in French.

It must be noted that, in all ten provinces, there are more people of English home language than of English mother tongue (this will be discussed in detail later, in chapter 9). However, there are fewer, sometimes far fewer, persons of French home language than of French mother tongue in all provinces except Quebec, where the numbers are approximately even. For this reason, francophones find it advantageous to cite the 'mother tongue' data, whereas anglos are better off using the figures based on the (newer) question on home language.

Ethnic origin is not a language question but will be the subject of a later section of this chapter, since it was once the only census question that could be used to distinguish 'French' from 'non-French.'

Requirements Set Out in Legislation

In 1867, the British North America Act was able to deal with bilingualism in one section. Section 133 merely stated that either the English or the French language might be used by any person in the federal Parliament or in the Quebec legislature, that the records and acts of those two bodies should be published in both languages, and that either language could be used in any court of Quebec or of Canada. In 1870, these provisions were extended to the newly created province of Manitoba, by section 23 of the Manitoba Act.

There was no requirement that individuals be provided with services in their own preferred official language, and the census of those early decades was not asked to distinguish between English-speakers and French-speakers.

The Official Languages Act was not passed until 1969, more than a century after Confederation. This act decreed that both English and French should be official languages of Canada and that bilingual districts should be established wherever the census found that, by the 'mother tongue' criterion, the linguistic minority was at least 10 per cent of the total population.

After two bilingual districts advisory boards had tried, and failed, to propose politically acceptable lists of bilingual districts, this particular notion was dropped and hence will not be found in Bill C-72 of 1988, which is now the Official Languages Act. None the less, the concept that members of the respective linguistic minority should be served in their own preferred language by offices of the federal government, whenever sufficient demand exists, continues to apply both to the English-speaking communities inside Quebec and to the French-speaking communities elsewhere in Canada. The problem is no longer one of concept, but has become the practical difficulty of defining 'sufficient demand.'

Adequacy of Census Data

The data now generated from the census are far more detailed than required by the Constitution Act (British North America Act) of 1867. However, the expectations of the respective minorities, to be served in their own language, have grown very rapidly in recent years, and the census questions can no longer suffice to supply the information now required. The chief statistician has admitted that the censuses have not included any specific question on first official language spoken and that the Official Languages Act of 1988 can be implemented only by use of estimates.[3]

It is possible to learn from the 1986 census data that approximately one-quarter of Canada's population are of French mother tongue, that about two-thirds are of English mother tongue, and that the others are of a wide variety of non-official mother tongues, from Cree to Chinese. The data also show that the proportion of francophones in Canada has declined since 1951 and that there has been an increasing polarization of the two official-language groups, with seven francophones of every eight now living in Quebec and with only one anglo of twenty-two to be found in that province.

At this point, however, there is a sharp divergence between the needs of those who use census data for research purposes and others who must implement federal or provincial legislation. Dr Fellegi, in

3 Ivan P. Fellegi, *Minutes* of the Joint Committee on Official Languages, 31 October 1989, 3:5

his prepared statement to the Joint Committee on Official Languages, referred to 'the complex reality of Canada' and stated that 'Statistics Canada's initiative [on interpretation of 1986 census data] is intended to more accurately reflect these complexities.'[4] Unfortunately, the solution proposed by Statistics Canada tends to favour the researcher, at the expense of the administrator.

To illustrate the problems faced by administrators of current legislation, consider the various numbers that can be assigned to the English-speaking minority in Quebec.

In 1986, only 580,030 persons (less than 9 per cent of the province's total population) gave the single response 'English' to the census question on mother tongue. This is the smallest number that can be used for the anglo minority of Quebec (interestingly, this proportion is cited by the Public Service Commission of Canada on page 31 of its annual report for 1987). However, several other numbers can be found in the census data, including:

- 676,050 persons gave the single response 'English' when asked what language they spoke the most often in their own homes;
- 789,985 persons gave a response to the 'mother tongue' question that included 'English'; and
- 917,155 persons gave a response to the 'home language' question that included 'English.'

In theory, Quebec's anglo minority could number anywhere from 580,030 to 917,155 persons, and, using the same methodology, the francophone minority outside Quebec and New Brunswick could number anywhere from 366,555 to 798,690 persons.

Recognizing the problems faced by potential users of these data, Statistics Canada has published two quite distinct attempts to reduce the confusion caused by multiple responses and other factors. The first of these, dated April 1988, stated that the English-speaking minority numbered 678,785 persons by the 'mother tongue' criterion and 796,695 persons by 'home language' (the corresponding figures for the French-speaking minorities outside Quebec and New Brunswick were 708,290 and 453,120, respectively).[5]

---

4 Ibid
5 Statistics Canada, *Adjusted Language Data* (Ottawa, April 1988)

Population Estimates by First Official Language Spoken

In September 1989, Statistics Canada published its second work, this one designed particularly 'to facilitate implementation of the Official Languages Act of 1988.' As Dr Fellegi stated to the joint committee, two series of estimates have been produced on the basis of information derived from the three linguistic questions of the 1986 census. The draft regulations tabled in the House of Commons on 8 November 1990 make specific reference to Method I of this publication.[6]

Using this method, the English-speaking minority of Quebec (after allocation, to either English or French, of those persons of non-official mother tongues) was calculated to consist of 858,325 persons (13.3 per cent of the province's population), a number high enough to satisfy most members of the minority. Using the same method, the French-speaking minority outside Quebec and New Brunswick was calculated to be 669,775 persons. The publication gives the size of the official-language minority in each census division and subdivision (municipality) of Canada, as well as in each of the twenty-five census metropolitan areas.

This is a major piece of work, done in an attempt to make up for the absence of a census question on the preferred official language of the respondent. Those using it should keep in mind that Treasury Board has chosen Method I, which gives priority to the 'mother tongue' over the (newer) 'home language' criterion and, as noted above, shows almost 670,000 French-speakers outside Quebec and New Brunswick; had Method II been chosen, giving priority to home language, the minority would number only 495,000.

By choosing Method I and by setting thresholds low enough that many areas are covered by the regulations that would not have been eligible for inclusion in the bilingual districts of the 1969 Official Languages Act, Treasury Board estimates that the proposals would cover 92 per cent of the French-speaking persons outside Quebec and 96 per cent of English-speaking persons in Quebec. This estimate and certain members' minority reports will be found in the minutes of the Joint Committee on Official Languages for 2 May 1991.

---

6 Draft of the proposed regulations respecting communications with and services to the public in either official language, tabled in accordance with section 85 of the Official Languages Act, 1990, section 2 (p. 1)

A Problem Caused by Multiple Responses

As noted in the previous chapter, there was an unusually high incidence of multiple response (e.g., 'English + French') to the 'home language' and 'mother tongue' questions of the 1986 census. These responses must be allocated to the two official languages but a practical problem will still remain: 1,000 'English + French' is not the same as 500 'English' plus 500 'French.' This problem is particularly sensitive because of a change in Statistics Canada's publication policies: at all earlier censuses, only the adjusted data had appeared in most tables, but the publications of the 1986 census showed the number of multiple responses received, highlighting their importance.

Non-official Languages

Although all 'allophones' – persons who are neither francophone nor anglophone – are often regarded as being similar, a special category must be mentioned: those who are Canadian citizens (by birth or by naturalization) and who have attended school in Canada. These persons have the right, under section 23 of the Charter of Rights and Freedoms, to send their children to minority-language schools if they themselves attended school in Canada in that language. The existing census data do not appear capable of differentiating such persons.

Ethnic Origin

'Ethnic origin' deserves special mention because it was, until the introduction of a question on mother tongue, the only census criterion that could be used to differentiate 'French' from other Canadians. Although never entirely valid as a measure of language preference, this criterion became of particularly dubious value whenever there had been a significant degree of interorigin marriage and/or of language mobility. This comment, it should be noted, applied in both directions, to the Irish orphans who were adopted by French-speaking foster parents in Quebec as well as to persons of French origin who settled in English-speaking areas of Canada.

An additional factor, which cannot be overlooked, is the recent sharp rise in frequency of multiple responses to the question on ethnic origin. At the 1986 census, only 18 million Canadians reported a single origin, while 7 million were shown as having two or more origins; the latter included one million persons with four or more origins each.

Changes in definitions and in editing procedures must also be noted. For example, in 1986, a person who reported his/her origin as 'English + Scottish' was counted as having given a multiple response; in 1981, however, the same answer would have been counted as a single response: 'British.'[7] This change in the editing procedures of Statistics Canada reduced the reported number of 'single origin British' from 9,674,245 in 1981 to only 6,332,725 in 1986, the remaining two or three million British being reported (and, incidentally, often hidden) among the multiple origins that were shown as a single line at the bottom of many of the tables published by Statistics Canada.

The Public Service Figures

A question may well be asked: If census data can cause such problems, how is it possible for the Public Service Commission of Canada to divide its employees, so neatly and completely, into 'anglophones' and 'francophones'?

The answer is that the commission does not use data from the census. The tables it publishes are made up from its own internal survey of employees (in most cases, using the Official Languages Information System) and are based on each person's expressed preference for one or the other of the two official languages. Multiple responses and replies that mention non-official languages are simply not accepted.

The 'Ideal' Census Question

It appears desirable for Statistics Canada to introduce a new census question, somewhat similar to the question used by the Public Service Commission. Responses to such a question would yield data enabling governments to implement legislation requiring that certain services be offered to the linguistic minorities. It might be noted that such a suggestion has been made even by the Fédération des francophones hors Québec.[8] To date, however, Statistics Canada has been unwilling to accept this suggestion.

---

7 'It should be noted that the British Only multiple responses included in the 1981 British single origins are, in 1986, listed as a multiple ethnic response': Statistics Canada, *Dictionary*, Catalogue no. 99-101E (Ottawa 1987), 14

8 Guy Matte (president, Fédération des francophones hors Québec), as reported in *Minutes* of the Joint Committee on Official Languages, 13 December 1990, 21:9

5

The Non-official Languages

By law, English and French are the official languages of Canada.[1] All other languages are non-official.

The non-official languages can be divided into two broad groups. The first group includes all the aboriginal languages, those of Canadian Indians and Inuit. The second is made up of the many languages brought to North America by immigrants from Europe, Asia, Africa, and elsewhere (excluding, of course, English and French).

Although there has long been a question on official languages spoken, not until 1991 did the census ask Canadians what, if any, non-official languages they could speak. As the results of this question will not be known until (probably) 1993, it is not yet possible to say that one non-official language is more popular than another.

However, the census has, for several decades, asked a question about each person's mother tongue, whether this be an official or a non-official language. Since 1971, a question about language most often spoken in the home has also been asked, although of only the sample population. Both the historical (1941 to 1981) and recent (1986) data are given in tables 2 and 3.

The historical data show that there has been a drastic change over the past few decades in the mother tongues of immigrants to Canada. The 1941 figures show only small numbers of persons reporting the languages of Asia and of Greece, Portugal, and Spain. By 1986, however, some of the once-common languages, such as Yiddish and Gaelic, had virtually disappeared, while Greek, Portuguese, and Spanish had

1 Official Languages Act, 1968–9, section 2; Constitution Act, 1982, section 16

TABLE 2
Recent historical development of some mother tongues, Canada, censuses of 1941, 1961, and 1981

	1941	1961	1981
Total population	11,506,655	18,238,247	24,343,181
English	6,488,190	10,660,534	14,918,460
French	3,354,753	5,123,151	6,249,100
Indian & Eskimo	130,939	166,531	146,290(?)[a]
German	322,228	563,713	522,855
Ukrainian	313,273	361,496	292,265
Scandinavian	143,917	116,714	67,725
Yiddish	129,806	82,448	32,760
Polish	128,711	161,720	127,960
Italian	80,260	339,626	528,775
Dutch	53,215	170,177	146,830
Magyar	46,287	85,939	83,720
Finnish	37,331	44,785	33,380
Chinese	33,500	49,099	224,030
Gaelic	32,708	7,533	2,790
Greek	8,747	40,455	122,960
Arabic	8,111	n/s[b]	50,115
Spanish	1,030	n/s	70,160
Portuguese	n/s	n/s	165,510
Punjabi	n/s	n/s	53,680

[a] (?) = does not include 20,285 persons who reported 'Indian' without specifying whether they meant 'North American Indian' or 'from the Indian subcontinent.'
[b] n/s = not shown in census page.

moved upwards on the list, and the number of persons speaking east-Asian languages (particularly Chinese, Punjabi, Vietnamese, and Tagalog) had considerably increased.

Technical Note re: Aboriginal Languages
The fact that a person is of a certain ethnic origin does not necessarily mean that he or she has any particular mother tongue or home language; language and origin can be quite different. This is true of aboriginals as well as of more recent immigrants and makes it difficult to state, with any assurance, the exact number of Indians, Inuit, or Métis in Canada.

The Métis have, of course, no associated mother tongue. In 1986,

TABLE 3
Some mother tongues and home languages of the population of Canada, 1986 (single responses only)[a]

	Mother tongue	Home language
Total single responses	24,354,390	23,862,330
English	15,334,085	16,595,535
French	6,159,740	5,798,470
N.A. Indian	117,010	79,712
Inuktitut	21,050	17,570
Italian	455,820	271,835
German	438,680	112,550
Chinese	266,560	230,480
Ukrainian	208,415	46,150
Portuguese	153,985	105,420
Dutch	123,670	14,430
Polish	123,120	55,150
Greek	110,350	72,550
Spanish	83,130	55,760
Hungarian	69,000	23,960
Punjabi	63,640	47,865
Tagalog	42,420	25,290
Vietnamese	41,560	40,345
Arabic	40,665	22,010
Yiddish	22,665	6,660
Gaelic	4,645	410

Sources: Mother tongue data – Statistics Canada, Language: Part 1, Catalogue no. 93-102 (Ottawa 1987), Table 1; home language data – Statistics Canada, Language: Part 2, Catalogue no. 93-103 (Ottawa 1989), Table 1

[a] There were 954,940 multiple responses to the mother tongue question, and 1,159,670 to the home language question.

the census found 59,745 persons who gave 'Métis'[2] as their single ethnic origin, most of them living in the three Prairie provinces. Almost three-quarters of these gave English as their mother tongue, just over 10 per cent gave French, 12 per cent reported a non-official language, and the remaining 8 per cent gave multiple responses.[3]

Of the 286,230 North American Indians, barely more than one-

2 Also spelled 'Metis'
3 Statistics Canada, Profile of Ethnic Groups, Catalogue no. 93-154 (Ottawa 1989), Table 2

third reported a non-official language and more than half English as the mother tongue; barely 5 per cent gave French, although 13 per cent lived in Quebec (these figures are for single responses only). The Inuit, living mainly in the Northwest Territories and the Ungava Peninsula, numbered only 27,285 (again, single origins only) but had a much higher rate of language retention: fewer than one in five reported English as their mother tongue, and only 750 gave French.

6

Natural Increase

Although birth rates have fallen drastically during the past three decades, the most important element of population growth in Canada is still natural increase, the excess of births over deaths. During the twelve months ending 31 December 1990, there were 399,270 live births and 193,470 deaths in the country, giving a natural increase of 205,800 for the year. During the same twelve months, net immigration was 174,574, the figure obtained by subtracting estimated emigration of 37,592 from the 212,166 immigrants received.[1]

While the actual number of deaths has risen, from 124,220 in 1950, Canada's death rate (per thousand population) has been steadily declining, and was 7.3 in 1990 as against 9.1 in 1950. Birth rates, however, have been subject to wide swings.

Canada's crude birth rate (live births per thousand population) fell during the depression years and touched a low of 20.1 in 1937. Recovery occurred during the 1940s, and a postwar peak of 28.9 was recorded in 1947; the rate remained above 27.0 until 1959. Then followed a sharp drop, to 19.4 by 1966, which continued on down to 15.5 by 1973. After a few years of seeming stability in the 15.3–15.5 range, the downward trend resumed, and a new low of 14.4 was reported in 1987. Despite increases in each of the next three years, preliminary data showed the birth rate at only 15.0 in 1990.

In the mid-1960s, the initial reaction to this drop in birth rates was to hypothesize that women were merely postponing having children.

---

1 Statistics Canada, *Quarterly Demographic Statistics*, Catalogue no. 91-002, vol. 4, no. 4 (April 1991) (data preliminary and subject to revision)

Even at a later date, when it had become evident that the size of families was being sharply reduced, politicians were unwilling to face up to the phenomenon and to its possible consequences. As recently as 1981, René Lévesque's 'natalist' electoral promises were denounced by nearly all feminists. Four years later, when Richard French chaired a (Quebec) provincial committee on population, the Conseil du statut de la femme told him: If there is a problem, solve it through immigration, not by natalist policies.[2]

In fairness to those who downplay the consequences of a drop in birth rates, it must be noted that, initially at least, the effects of fewer children can appear beneficial. No longer is it necessary to build additional schools and pay ever-increasing education taxes; no longer are women tied to the home and unable to take an outside job. It is only in the long term that adverse effects begin to appear: unless immigration fills the gap, there will be fewer people of working age to support an increasing number of older people. The latter, it must be noted, are now living longer and the cost of supporting them is rising. The savings realized through a smaller number of children will be more than dissipated in payments related to the aged.

Birth rates have been dropping throughout the developed world, in Japan as well as in Europe and North America, and are now at levels below those required for replacement of the generations. In Canada, there is a special problem, since low birth rates have already begun to affect seriously the former balance between the two official-language groups.

Until the late 1950s, birth rates of French-speaking families throughout Canada were sufficiently high to balance the effects of both immigration and anglicization. However, during the subsequent three decades, the birth rates of the French-speaking communities fell faster, and to lower levels, than did those of the non-French. In consequence, the proportion of French-speakers in Canada's population dropped from the traditional 30 per cent to a 1986 level of only 24 per cent, with further declines probable.

Réjean Lachapelle found that the fertility rates of women of French mother tongue were down to levels below those of women of English mother tongue in the three provinces examined: Quebec, Ontario,

---

2 Louis Falardeau, 'La dénatalité: Un sujet délicat dont les gouvernements n'aiment pas parler,' La Presse, 10 September 1988, B1

TABLE 4
Number of children in Canada aged 0 to 4 years, total and by mother tongue, censuses of 1951 to 1986[a]

Census year	Total	English	French	Other
1951	1,722	1,060	558	104
1961	2,256	1,411	660	185
1971	1,815	1,185	458	172
1986	1,810	1,271	418	121

Notes
All figures have been rounded to the nearest thousand.
Mother tongue has been used, instead of home language, to provide a longer historical series; for this age group, there is minimal difference between mother tongue and home language.
The 1951 census was the first to include Newfoundland.
For 1986, Table 3 of census publication *Language: Part 1* (Catalogue no. 93-102) was used, with multiple responses allocated by the author.

and New Brunswick.[3] As Lachapelle worked from fertility rates, a more scientific measure than crude birth rates, his conclusion is of particular significance: the decreasing size of French-speaking families is an important factor in the decline of francophones as a proportion of Canada's population.

The effect of falling birth rates can be seen from table 4, which shows that almost one-third of Canada's youngest inhabitants were of French mother tongue in 1951 but that the proportion had dropped to less than one-quarter by 1986. At that lower level, it should be noted, the number of births to francophone families was below the minimum required to maintain the relative strength of the French-speaking minority in Canada, with no surplus to compensate for the historically adverse effects of immigration and anglicization.

Incidentally, it should be noted (see table 4) that the actual number of children with French as their mother tongue was 25 per cent lower in 1986 than it had been in 1951, although the number of children with English as their mother tongue had increased by 20 per cent during the same thirty-five years.

During each of the three years from 1988 to 1990, there was a small but noteworthy recovery in the number of births reported for Quebec, which will, almost certainly, be reflected in a corresponding

3 Réjean Lachapelle, 'Changes in Fertility among Canada's Linguistic Groups,' *Canadian Social Trends*, Autumn 1988, 2–8

recovery in the number of births to Canada's French-speaking families. However, the future could be quite dark for those who are concerned about the declining proportion of francophones in Canada's population.

The children born in Canada now come (chiefly) from mothers in the 20–39 age group. In 1986, there were 1,152,600 women of French mother tongue in this age group; in sharp contrast, there were only 858,900 in the group aged 0–19 in 1986, those who are the potential mothers of the year 2006.[4]

Thus, the francophone proportion of Canada's population appears destined to continue its downward trend, over at least the next two decades. The trend will be reversed only if French birth rates suddenly (and quite unexpectedly) climb to well above their present levels and/ or if there is a higher proportion of francophones (or *'francophonisables'*) among future immigrants.

Marriages

Postponement of (or, even forgoing) marriage was once a common form of birth control. In recent years, however, there has been a sharply increasing incidence of births to women shown as 'never married.'[5]

This last statement must be qualified by noting that, even within Statistics Canada, there have been differences of opinion as to what constitutes marriage. The annual figures put out by the federal government show as 'married' only those women who have been through a religious or civil ceremony; the census, however, is willing to include all those persons who are currently living with a common-law partner.[6]

In any case, the message is clear: the number of marriages reported in a year does not permit an accurate forecast of the number of births to be expected in subsequent years.

Incidentally, the census formerly asked only married women (as so defined in the census) to report the number of live births that they had produced during their lifetimes. In the 1991 census, there was a

---

4 Statistics Canada, *Language: Part 1*, Catalogue no. 93-102 (Ottawa 1987), Table 3

5 Bureau de la statistique du Québec, *La situation démographique au Québec*, 1990 edition (Quebec City 1991), Figure 5.13 (a striking graph for the Province of Quebec)

6 Statistics Canada, *Postcensal Annual Estimates of Population ...*, Catalogue no. 91-210 (Ottawa 1990), vol. 8, 19

significant change, and the question (Q. 23) was, following the U.S. practice, addressed to all women, regardless of their marital status. The change means, for example, that it will, in the future, be possible to see whether there has been a selective out-movement from Quebec of anglos who had decided to begin their families, which could be useful information.

Quebec

The first section of this chapter described the situation as it applied to all of Canada. However, since the great majority of French-speakers live within the Province of Quebec, the drop in French birth rates has been accompanied by a related problem: the decline in relative importance of Quebec's population, from almost 29 per cent to barely more than 25 per cent of Canada's population.

These two problems had been foreseen by Quebec demographers: Professor Jacques Henripin, for example, asked in 1974 that the provincial government adopt 'natalist policies' to encourage a return to larger families.[7]

At the 1951 census, the first to include data from Newfoundland, Quebec held almost 29 per cent of Canada's population. By 1986, Quebec's relative strength was down to 25.8 per cent, and estimates made at the beginning of 1991 showed a proportion of just under 25.4 per cent.

Admittedly, Quebec has been suffering a net loss in interprovincial migration, while it is attracting (and holding) far fewer than its proper share of international immigrants. However, the decline in births is a key factor: during 1986 and 1987, the number of births in Quebec was below 85,000 for the first time since 1940 (a year when the population of the province had been only 3.3 million). Despite the recovery noted in 1988–90, Quebec's birth rate has not yet returned to a level above that of the rest of Canada, the situation prevailing until 1959.

Although no effort is being made to encourage larger French-speaking families outside Quebec, the government of that province is attempting to at least maintain the relative population of Quebec at the present level, relative to the population of Canada. To encourage Quebec women to bear more children, the provincial budget

---

7 Jacques Henripin, 'Faut-il tenter d'accroître la fécondité au Québec?' *Bulletin de l'Association des démographes au Québec* (Montreal, November 1974), 92ff

of May 1988 included a package of measures intended to reward the mothers of large families. An important feature was the promise to pay a cash bonus of $3,000 after birth of a third child, the amount raised at each successive budget and now (mid-1991) standing at $7,500.

The fundamental problem remains: for each individual woman, a significant consequence of having fewer children is that she is freer to improve her own status. There is a conflict between this personal objective and the need for the collectivity to perpetuate itself by producing more children. At present, and despite the upturn in birth rates noted since 1987, the former objective appears to be dominant.

7

Immigration

The 1986 census reported 3.9 million immigrants then living in Canada, slightly less than 16 per cent of the country's total population. Of these, the great majority had arrived since 1945, and only a few people remained of the vast waves of immigrants who had come to Canada during the first half of this century and who, during the period 1911 to 1931, made up just over 22 per cent of Canada's population (see table 19 in Appendix A).

Although only one Canadian in six was born abroad, everyone now in Canada is either an immigrant or the descendant of immigrants. The remark has been derided as being 'trivial,' but it expresses a significant fact that is often disregarded by those discussing immigration and its effects on the Canadian population.

Should someone moving from the British Isles to Canada be called an immigrant? The term seems correct, since there was an 'Office of Her Majesty's Chief Agent for the Superintendence of Emigration to Canada' in the nineteenth century, well before Canada became an independent country.

However, even if agreement can be reached on terminology, there remain several problems of a technical nature. One of these is the question of whether (how) to count persons who moved from Newfoundland to Canada prior to 1949. A considerably more important problem is how to quantify immigration.

Probably the most common way to measure immigration is simply to count the number of persons arriving at ports of entry. Statistics are readily available to show the number of immigrants who have arrived in Canada each year; these data usually give sex, age, country of birth, citizenship, etc. For example, some 4.9 million foreign-born persons arrived in Canada between 1945 and 1981.

Other methods of measuring immigration may also be used, and these (generally) give results that are lower than those obtained by the method described above. For example, the 1981 census found 3.3 million foreign-born persons in Canada who had entered the country since 1945. Allowing for mortality, this finding suggests that about one-quarter of all those counted as being in Canada had actually moved out again, either returning to their country of birth or moving on to another country.

A third method takes the estimated number of persons moving out of Canada, including native-born as well as foreign-born, and deducts this number from that of foreign-born received to produce the figure for 'net immigration.' Continuing with the example cited in the previous two paragraphs, net immigration for the period 1945 to 1981 was 2.7 million, the result obtained by subtracting the estimated 2.28 million emigrants from the 4.95 million arrivals (the number of emigrants must be estimated, a process naturally subject to possible inaccuracy, since no record is kept of persons moving out of Canada).

The three methods just described permit the statement that immigration into Canada during the period 1945 to 1981 was 4.9 million, 3.3 million, or 2.7 million; any one of these figures may be cited, depending on the method of calculation preferred.

The countries of origin of immigrants may be as important as the actual numbers coming into Canada. Two centuries ago, new arrivals came chiefly from western and northern Europe. By the beginning of the present century, many immigrants reported birthplaces in eastern and southern Europe. After 1971, India and southeast Asia appeared among the top-ten areas, while Jamaica and Guyana were also on this list, despite their own relatively small populations.

In 1986 and 1987, over 40 per cent of all immigrants were from Asia and only 24 per cent were from Europe, including the United Kingdom and Ireland. The Caribbean islands and the countries of Central and South America contributed one-fifth of the almost 250,000 foreign-born persons received during those two years; only 6 per cent came from the United States, and the remainder came from Africa, Oceania, and elsewhere.

The 1986 census reported 3.9 million immigrants in Canada. Of these, 2.1 million (53 per cent) were in Ontario, including 1,233,095 in the Toronto census metropolitan area (CMA). Quebec was home to only 527,135 immigrants (13.5 per cent of the total), most of them being in the Montreal area. Vancouver was the third most important magnet for immigrants, with 391,845 living within its CMA. These figures, it should be noted, do not include the children of immigrants.

Toronto's population was 36 per cent foreign-born; Vancouver's was 29 per cent. Other major metropolitan areas were in the 17–21 per cent range but there were exceptions: Hamilton, at 24 per cent, and Montreal, at 16 per cent, were just outside the common range, while Halifax had only 7 per cent immigrants among its population and Quebec City came a poor last, at only 2 per cent.[1]

Regardless of their intended destination, and although there were, of course, many exceptions, the great majority of immigrants arriving in Canada since 1760 have adopted the English language, even if they did not speak it on arrival. The 1986 census reported that French was the home language of only about 5 per cent of all foreign-born residents of Canada, compared with 27 per cent among native-born Canadians.[2] Perhaps of even greater significance, of the 3.7 million immigrants to Canada who claimed to be able to converse in either English or French, 83.7 per cent spoke 'English only,' 12.7 per cent spoke both official languages, and a mere 3.6 per cent spoke 'French only.'

The consequence has been that immigration favours the English-speaking component of Canada's population. When net immigration was high, the proportion of francophones in Canada declined; when net immigration slowed, history shows that the relatively high natural increase of French-speaking families tended to restore the old proportion.

It is important to note that the previous paragraph referred to 'net immigration.' Between 1860 and 1900, more than 1.7 million arrivals were counted at Canadian ports of entry, so gross immigration was reasonably high, considering the country's average population of less than 5 million. However, during the same forty years, an estimated 2 million people moved out of Canada, chiefly to the United States, with the result that net immigration was actually negative; there were only 699,000 foreign-born persons counted by the 1901 census.

Although many French Canadians were among those who moved

1 All data are from Statistics Canada, *Census Metropolitan Areas and Census Agglomerations: Part 2*, Catalogue no. 94-128 (Ottawa 1988).
2 Statistics Canada, *Profile of the Immigrant Population*, Catalogue no. 93-155 (Ottawa 1989), Table 1

southward (see chapter 11), the majority of those who left this country were English-speaking. In consequence, the end of the century saw persons of French origin at 30.7 per cent of the total population of Canada, a proportion slightly higher than the 30.0 per cent of 1881.

After the Prairies had been opened to colonization, at the end of the last century, heavy net immigration into Canada resumed. In the decade from 1903 to 1912, 2.2 million new arrivals were counted, and an additional 400,870 were received in 1913, the highest figure for a single year on record. This occurred, it should be noted, at a time when the population of Canada was considerably less than one-third of today's figure.

Immigration fell off sharply during the wartime years, but the census taken in 1921 found two million foreign-born persons living in Canada, just over 22 per cent of the total population. At that census, persons of French origin were down to only 27.9 per cent of Canada's population, the lowest proportion since Confederation, and 'alarms were sounded' by Abbé Groulx and Quebec's Action française.[3]

The 1920s saw further heavy immigration, but this was largely offset by emigration and by mortality. During the decade, 1.2 million foreign-born persons were counted into Canada, but the census of 1931 found that the number of those born outside the country had increased by only 352,000 since 1921. The decade of the depression, which followed, saw immigration plummet, to an average of only 14,000 persons per year, and new arrivals were even rarer during the war years. By 1951, fewer than 15 per cent of Canadians reported foreign birth.

As noted above, the French element of Canada's population benefited from the drop in immigration. Despite Newfoundland's entry into the census data, persons of French origin made up 30.8 per cent of Canada's population at the census of 1951, the highest proportion since 1871.[4]

However, significant immigration resumed after the end of the war, and 125,414 foreign-born were counted into Canada in 1948, a level not previously seen since the late 1920s. As noted earlier in this chapter, total postwar immigration had reached 4.9 million persons by 1981. There followed a four-year lull, during which barely more

3 Susan Mann Trofimenkoff, *The Dream of Nation* (Toronto: Macmillan of Canada 1982), 222
4 Note that the reference on page 17 was to persons of French mother tongue.

than 90,000 immigrants per year were allowed into the country, but newcomers are now arriving at the rate of about 200,000 annually.

During the entire postwar period, from the beginning of 1946 until the end of 1989, Canada received some six million immigrants. This averages just under 136,000 persons per year, well below the 237,000 per year who arrived in the period 1903 to 1913, and only 0.7 per cent of the average population during the postwar period. However, given the decline in birth rates, even this number has been sufficient to cause a decline in the proportion of French-speakers among Canada's population.

It seems probable that immigration quotas will increase during the next few years. If future immigrants favour the English language, as have those in the past, then the French-speaking proportion of Canada's population will continue to decrease. Incidentally, and with only a few exceptions, the country of origin of immigrants does not seem to be a major factor in their choice of language after arrival in Canada. For example, only 15 per cent of those born in Portugal and 23 per cent of those born in Italy have come to Quebec; the remainder have settled elsewhere in Canada, chiefly in Ontario, and the second language for them is English, not French.

Immigration into Quebec

The 1986 census reported that 69 per cent of those immigrants living in Quebec claimed to be able to converse in French, compared to only 7 per cent of those living outside Quebec. This finding suggests that it is important to Quebec's majority-language group that as high as possible a number of Canada's immigrants be persuaded to settle in the one province in which new arrivals are exposed to the French language in school, at work, and even in the home.

The provinces, including Quebec, have the right to make laws in relation to immigration 'as far only as [such a law] is not repugnant to any act of the Parliament of Canada.'[5] In other words, the federal and provincial governments share authority in this area, subject to the paramountcy of federal power.

The Cullen-Couture Agreement of 1979 gave Quebec a limited role in determining Canadian immigration policy. This role would have been considerably extended had the Meech Lake Accord been ratified.

5 The Constitution Act (originally, the British North America Act), 1867, section 95

A federal-provincial communiqué dated 30 April 1987 stated that Quebec would be 'guaranteed' an annual number of immigrants, including refugees, proportional to its share of the population of Canada, with the right to exceed this figure by 5 per cent. This means that Quebec would have been 'guaranteed' 26 to 27 per cent of all newcomers to Canada.

This proportion is about double the historical level. Annual figures show that 1967 was the most recent year during which 20 per cent of Canada's immigrants named Quebec as their intended province of initial destination.[6] The same (provincial) source shows that only 17.7 per cent of Canada's 1985–9 immigrants named Quebec.

An independent source of data, the census, gives a picture that is even more pessimistic regarding Quebec's historical ability to attract and hold newcomers from abroad. The 1986 census reported that Quebec was home to only 13.9 per cent of all immigrants who had reported a date of arrival in Canada between 1946 and mid-1986, although approximately 29 per cent of Canada's population lived in Quebec at the beginning of that period.[7]

Incidentally, the annual figures, showing the number of immigrants destined for each province, are based on the declarations made by the immigrants themselves at the time they enter Canada. There does not appear to be any follow-up to verify the correctness of these declarations. One newspaper article actually began: 'Hundreds of wealthy immigrants from Asia have been given special visas by Quebec but are heading for other provinces once they arrive in Canada.'[8]

However, disregarding this factor, which may be minor, Quebec does seem to be facing two quite distinct problems. On the one hand, the provincial government must do its best to attract newcomers who, in the face of a falling birth rate, will maintain the province's political weight within Canada. On the other hand, care must be taken to seek immigrants who will integrate into the language of the province's majority; events occurring in 1990–1 on the Island of Montreal show the danger of admitting persons who prefer another language.

The 1986 census showed that only 29 per cent of the 527,130 foreign-born persons living in Quebec reported French as the language they were then speaking most frequently in their homes, well

6 Bureau de la statistique du Québec, *La situation démographique au Québec*, 1990 edition (Quebec City 1991), Table 602
7 Statistics Canada, *Profile of the Immigrant Population*, Tables 1 and 6
8 *Ottawa Citizen*, 8 August 1988, A3

TABLE 5
Official languages spoken by the foreign-born population
of Quebec, censuses of 1951, 1971, and 1986 (percentages)

Languages spoken	1951	1971	1986
French only	9	18	24
French + English	29	35	45
English only	57	39	25
Neither	5	8	6

below the 88 per cent reporting French, among those born in Canada (including, of course, the children of immigrants).[9]

This said, it must be noted that, in recent decades, there has been a significant upward trend in the proportion of immigrants who adopt French as their home language. Directly related to this, the proportion of foreign-born living in Quebec who claim the ability to converse in French has risen from 38 per cent in 1951 to 69 per cent in 1986, while those claiming English has fallen from 86 per cent to 70 per cent (see table 5).

This trend is partly attributable to the departure from Quebec of many of those persons who preferred to speak English. However, at least two other factors must be mentioned: a / there has been a marked change in the countries of origin of immigrants and in their language characteristics; and b / there is an increasing pressure on immigrants in Quebec to speak the language of the province's majority, and the children of immigrants, even those of English mother tongue, are now obliged, with only a few exceptions, to attend French-language schools.

It is far from certain, however, that immigration can ever make up for the babies who are no longer being born to French-speaking families: 'Il suffit de faire le calcul du nombre d'immigrants qu'il faudrait ... pour constater l'illusion d'une telle panacée.'[10]

9 Statistics Canada, *Profile of the Immigrant Population*, Table 6 (multiple responses distributed)
10 Michel Paillé, 'L'immigration massive: Une panacée à la dépopulation du Québec?' *Bulletin du Conseil de la langue française*, Autumn 1986, 7

8

Interprovincial Migration

Historically, interprovincial migration was an effective way of bringing English-speakers into Quebec and of spreading French-speakers
throughout the rest of Canada. In 1971, for example, 17 per cent of
Quebec's anglos had been born in other parts of Canada. At that same
census, 27 per cent of Ontario's francophones had been born in other
provinces, most of them in Quebec, while no fewer than 65 per cent
of the francophones living in British Columbia had been born elsewhere in Canada, about half of them in Quebec.[1]

Réjean Lachapelle has stated that the survival of the French-speaking communities in western Canada, in southern Ontario, and in the
Atlantic region depends on continuing francophone migration into
those areas, from Quebec or elsewhere.[2] Meanwhile, the vitality of
Quebec's anglo minority is suffering from a net out-migration that is
particularly affecting its younger people.

In the past, migration of French Canadians was often encouraged
by 'colonization societies' and by companies seeking low-cost labour
(Maillardville, in British Columbia, was set up by the Fraser Mills
Lumber Company). Now, however, only the federal government seems
to be promoting the movement of francophones into predominantly
English-speaking areas, and the limited efforts that are being made
in this direction are offset by the departure of francophones from the

---

1 Statistics Canada, *Language and Age by Birthplace*, Catalogue no. 92-739 (Ottawa
  1974), Table 32
2 Réjean Lachapelle, 'La démolinguistique et le destin des minorités françaises vi-
  vant à l'extérieur du Québec,' *Mémoires de la Société royale du Canada*, 5th series,
  vol. 1 (1986), 137

minority communities (a recent example is our former governor general, Jeanne Sauvé, who was born in Saskatchewan but now lives in Quebec).

The importance of interprovincial migration might lead one to expect that such migration is carefully documented and that full and accurate data are available for study. Regrettably, this is not the case.

Under Canadian law (subsection 6[2] of the Charter of Rights and Freedoms), there is no barrier to interprovincial migration; that is, every resident of Canada may move freely from one part of the country to another. No records are kept of such movements, and the numbers commonly quoted for annual migration are based chiefly on change-of-address notices received by the family-allowance offices. Although these data are refined through use of information from other sources, primarily the addresses used on personal income tax forms, they are still of somewhat lower quality than might be desired.

Quebec's Bureau de la statistique has noted that the preliminary and revised figures for interprovincial migration can differ by a considerable percentage and that this discrepancy causes problems for anyone attempting to analyse the internal migration of Canadians.[3] In any case, the annual estimates provide no details of those moving, apart from the number of persons involved and the official language in which the change-of-address notices were written.

The quinquennial census is an alternative source of data. This census asks a sample of all Canadians to state their place of residence five years earlier. If the answer is in a province different from that in which the respondent currently resides, then he or she is counted as having made an interprovincial move. Statistics Canada is then able to produce profiles of the movers, showing their age, sex, language group, etc.

The data collected by the census should provide a reliable account of interprovincial migration. However, these census data tend to understate the number of moves that have taken place, since they do not record any of the following:

– persons who are less than five years old at census date and who are not asked to reply to the 'previous residence' question;

3 Bureau de la statistique du Québec, *La situation démographique au Québec*, 1988 edition (Quebec City 1988), 84

- persons who had moved to another province and then departed from Canada;
- persons who had moved to another province but who had died before the census was taken;
- persons who had moved to another province and then had moved back to their original province, all within the five-year intercensal period; and
- anyone who had 'forgotten' that he or she had been living in a different province five years earlier.

Also, only one move would be counted per person, although some people may make two or more interprovincial moves during any five-year period.

These varied omissions can add up to a substantial total. For example, the number of departures from Quebec for the five-year period 1981–6 was 197,113, while the number of interprovincial migrants shown by the 1986 census as having been in Quebec five years earlier was only 130,200, or 34 per cent less. The size of the gap between the two numbers shows that they cannot be used interchangeably. It is probable that use of the census figure gravely understates the magnitude of interprovincial migration, particularly since even the annual estimates may be on the low side.

If the data available from the census considerably understate the number of interprovincial moves, why are they cited so frequently? The answer can be found above: use of census data permits preparation of detailed profiles of the movers, and these profiles are eagerly sought by users of census material.

A good example of the type of profile that can be prepared is found in a recent report by Mireille Baillargeon, of the Ministère des communautés culturelles et de l'immigration du Québec.[4] Table III.14 of this report shows that, of the 203,040 persons counted elsewhere in Canada in 1981 but who had been living in Quebec five years earlier, only 39,075 had reported French as the language they spoke most often at home. In other words, although non-francophones make up less than one-fifth of the population of Quebec, they represented more than four-fifths of all those known to have moved out of the province between 1976 and 1981.

4 'L'évolution et les caractéristiques linguistiques des échanges migratoires interprovinciaux et internationaux du Québec depuis 1971,' L'état de la langue française au Québec (Quebec City: Conseil de la langue française 1986), 127ff

This sort of information, even if it is based on an incomplete reporting of the migrants, is of fundamental importance to anyone studying the evolution of Canada's official-language minorities. It suggests that interprovincial migration is no longer promoting a blending of Canada's two major language groups and that, on the contrary, recent migration has actually been acting to increase polarization, with those who prefer to use the English language moving out of Quebec and with francophones tending to concentrate within the province.

Supporting this hypothesis, a report prepared for the Quebec government in 1991 calls attention to the fact that, regardless of the legal aspects (all citizens of Canada are free to circulate throughout Canada), there is a cost involved, related to language, for the French-speaker who moves out of Quebec.[5] The same comment would, of course, be applicable to the English-speaker considering a move into Quebec.

In summary, interprovincial migration has played an important role in the past in building up and, later, revitalizing Canada's various minority-language communities. More recently, however, its character has changed, and it may now be one of the factors promoting linguistic polarization.

---

5 Commission on the Political and Constitutional Future of Quebec, *Report* (Bélanger-Campeau Report) (Quebec City 1991), 25 (French-language version)

9

Anglicization

Although this chapter might have been entitled 'Language Transfer,' its actual title appears to reflect more accurately the present situation. Most of this country's immigrants have adopted the language used almost everywhere north of the Rio Grande. At the time of the 1986 census, just over 83 per cent of Canada's population claimed to be able to carry on a conversation in English, and the proportion was over 98 per cent for those living outside Quebec and northern New Brunswick.

Regarding other language criteria, the 1986 census states that 1,112,830 Canadians of non-official mother tongues reported English as the language they were speaking most often in their own homes, compared to only 31,685 who reported French.[1] Among these residents of Canada, English has been favoured over French by a margin of approximately thirty-five to one.

Even within Quebec, the one province in which French is the majority language, persons of non-official mother tongues who had transferred to an official home language favoured English over French by a margin of seven to three. Outside Quebec, only 2,330 persons of non-official mother tongues reported French as their home language, compared to 1,039,565 who reported English.

However, not only persons of non-official mother tongues have adopted English as the language of their homes. Of at least equal

---

1 These numbers, and those in the next paragraph, are the single responses given at the 1986 census. Detailed data for both 1981 and 1986 may be found in Statistics Canada, *Language Retention and Transfer*, Catalogue no. 93-153 (Ottawa 1989).

concern to francophones has been the extent to which the transfers from French to English exceed those in the other direction. Outside Quebec and New Brunswick, in 1986, there were 708,290 persons of French mother tongue but only 453,120 who reported French as the language they spoke in their homes (both figures determined by Statistics Canada after allocation of all multiple responses).

It is, of course, possible to cite individual cases in which a person of English or of non-official mother tongue may now be speaking French in his or her own home. However, these cases appear to be relatively small in number, in comparison with those in which persons of French mother tongue have adopted English as their home language.

Although some recent studies claim that the process is slowing,[2] many of the French-speaking communities have been seriously eroded by the progressive anglicization of their members. This is occurring with particular frequency when there are many linguistically mixed marriages; in an area where the usual language is English, it is rare that the children of a French-English marriage would grow up as francophones.[3]

Northern New Brunswick and the east and north of Ontario must be regarded as special cases in that many of their francophones live in areas where French is the majority language. In such areas, there is a relatively low rate of net anglicization.

In other areas, particularly in certain cities, there has been a quite different factor at work to reduce the apparent rate of anglicization of persons of French mother tongue. To quote from a telephone survey made public in 1986, over 80 per cent of the French-speaking population of Toronto had been born outside Ontario, and many of them expected to return to Quebec within a very few years.[4] Evidently, such people are able to retain the French language.

Regarding the seven provinces and two territories west of Ontario

2 Réjean Lachapelle, 'Evolution of Language Groups and the Official Languages Situation in Canada,' paper presented to the American Sociological Association, San Francisco, 1989
3 Charles Castonguay has stressed the importance of linguistically mixed marriages in promoting anglicization. See, for example, his testimony to the Standing Joint Committee on Official Languages, 12 March 1986, *Minutes*, 25:7 and 25:8.
4 François Brousseau, 'Les Franco-Torontois en chiffres,' *Le Droit*, 4 January 1988, 18

and east of New Brunswick, the 1986 census found only 84,935 persons who reported French as the language they spoke most often in their own homes, plus 53,655 who reported that they spoke both English and French. These figures should be compared with the 192,175 who gave French as their reply to the 'mother tongue' question, plus the 49,535 who claimed that their mother tongue was 'English + French.'[5] Regardless of the way in which the multiple responses are treated, it appears clear that, as francophones move away from the Quebec border, they can have little hope of hearing the French language spoken by their grandchildren.

The losses suffered elsewhere in Canada have not been made up by gains within Quebec. On the contrary, the 1986 census reported that there were actually fewer persons of French home language than of French mother tongue in the one province in which French is the majority language.[6] This indicates that the number of transfers of persons of non-official mother tongues (chiefly, immigrants and their children) to French home language had not even made up for the net loss, towards English home language, of persons of French mother tongue.

Anglicization has already affected many of the third- and fourth-generation Franco-Americans, the grandchildren and great-grandchildren of those francophones who migrated southwards into the mill towns of New England. It has significantly reduced the proportion of French-speakers in Atlantic and western Canada and is noticeable even in such border cities as Ottawa and Moncton.

The greater availability of minority-language schools outside Quebec and the recent laws forbidding almost all immigrants living in Quebec from sending their children to English-language schools will certainly have some effect in slowing the rate of anglicization in Canada.

None the less, it seems probable that, except in Quebec and northern New Brunswick, there is no realistic expectation that anglicization can be eliminated as a factor leading to the disappearance of the French language. Rural isolation, which once protected many of the minority-language colonies, no longer exists, destroyed by the elec-

5 Statistics Canada, *Language Retention and Transfer*
6 The difference is slight. However, it can be seen either from the single responses of ibid, or in Statistics Canada, *Adjusted Language Data* (Ottawa, April 1988).

tronic media and the automobile. The recent weakening of religious boundaries must also be noted, since this, too, is a factor leading to more mixed marriages.

10

Minority-Language Schools

At the time of Confederation, religion, in its sectarian sense, was of considerable importance to most Canadians. Reflecting this, section 93 of the British North America Act, passed in 1867 by the Parliament at Westminster, placed specific obligations and restrictions on the provinces of Quebec and Ontario with regard to 'Separate or Dissentient Schools.' Section 22 of the Manitoba Act, passed in 1870, also protected denominational boards.

In contrast to this demonstrated concern for religion, no reference was made in either act to the language or languages that should be used in the schools. Although there have always been English-language schools in Quebec and French-language schools outside Quebec, these often existed only by a form of benign neglect.

In the mid-1800s, schools were small and so closely related to the local parish church that religious guarantees may have been expected to provide language guarantees. However, there was no identification of religion with language on any scale above that of the parish.

According to the 1861 census, the latest available to the Fathers of Confederation, there were 258,141 members of the 'Church of Rome' in Upper Canada, but only 35,676 persons of French origin. In other words, not quite one Catholic in seven was French in what is now Ontario. In Lower Canada, the identification of 'English-speaking' with 'Protestant' was closer than that of 'French' with 'Catholic' in Ontario, but the two terms were still far from being interchangeable.[1]

By the 1980s, however, the emphasis had shifted to language, and

1 Cf. letter by former senator Eugene Forsey, in the *Globe and Mail*, 4 March 1987.

the importance of religion had waned considerably. Of particular relevance to the legislation, the absence of French-language schools in several areas outside Quebec was being blamed for the high rates of anglicization found in those areas.

For these reasons, the Constitution Act of 1982 is silent on the question of religion in the schools, but provides extensive guarantees for minority-language schooling. Section 23 of the Charter of Rights and Freedoms, a part of the act, states that certain citizens have the right to send their children to schools of the minority language – English in Quebec, French elsewhere.

Section 23 has several peculiar features. Not the least of these is the fact that the constitutional right to attend minority schools is given through the parents or, in some cases, through brothers and sisters. Nowhere in the charter is it required that the prospective pupil have even the slightest familiarity with the minority language.

Another aspect worth noting is that section 23 is not symmetrical. No matter where they live in Canada, citizens of French mother tongue, including naturalized immigrants, have been given, by paragraph 23(1)(a), the constitutional right to send their children to French-language schools, numbers permitting. In contrast, section 59 of the charter states that paragraph 23(1)(a) does not apply to citizens of English mother tongue in Quebec, until (and unless) the provincial government so decrees. Criticism of this asymmetry began as early as November 1981, and, more recently, after seven years of inaction on the part of the Quebec government, a private member's bill was actually introduced in an unsuccessful attempt to repeal section 59.[2]

Despite the continuing existence of section 59, paragraph 23(1)(b) and subsection 23(2) of the charter have been in effect in Quebec and have enabled a number of children to attend English-language schools. In 1982, Chief Justice Jules Deschênes, in a decision of the Superior Court of Quebec, stated that the charter took precedence over Quebec's Bill 101; the latter would have restricted access to minority-language schools to children of parents who had attended English-language schools in Quebec and would have forced into French-language schools the children of parents educated in English in other parts of Canada (the 'Quebec Clause' vs. the 'Canada Clause'). This judgment was upheld by the Supreme Court of Canada in 1984.[3]

2 *Hansard*, 2 May 1989, 1224–34
3 A.G. Que. v. *Association of Protestant School Boards* [1984] 2 SCR 66

It must be emphasized that nothing prevents a province from enacting legislation that goes beyond the minimum requirements of the charter. Ontario did this in 1988, when its Bill 109 waived the charter restriction on 'sufficient number' (subsection 23[3]) and also added a fourth category to those eligible for admission to schools of the linguistic minority: anyone (regardless of family background) who can obtain approval from an admissions committee.[4]

Two Opposing Philosophies of Admission
Although the fact is seldom highlighted, there exist two quite-opposed points of view as to the ideal composition of the student body attending minority-language schools.

At one extreme will be found those who wish to restrict admission to convinced members of the linguistic minority. Although sometimes referred to (pejoratively) as 'élitist,' this point of view reflects the belief that only a homogeneous, devoted group of students and parents can ensure that their schools will produce graduates who are thoroughly competent in the minority language and that these schools will also serve as centres for the various activities of the minority-language community. An example of this attitude can be cited from 1977, when l'École Charlebois, in Ottawa, insisted on the exclusive use of French by students at all times when they were on school grounds. An editorial praising this action appeared in the French-language local newspaper.[5]

At the other extreme (there are, of course, intermediate positions) are those who seek to maximize the number of students enrolled in the minority-language schools. This philosophy appears to have guided the drafting of section 23 of the Charter of Rights and Freedoms. Michel Paillé, of Quebec's Conseil de la langue française, reports that, in Canada outside Quebec and New Brunswick, there are 214,583 persons of school age who have the constitutional right to attend French-language schools because they have at least one parent who is of French mother tongue; this figure far exceeds the 91,757 persons aged 6 to 17 who reported either 'French' or 'English + French' as their mother tongue in 1986.[6]

As one of the possible consequences of section 23, nominally French

---

4 Subsection 11(3) of Ontario's Bill 109 (1988)
5 Guy Lacombe, 'L'école Charlebois donne le ton!' Le Droit, 17 February 1977, 6
6 Michel Paillé, Les écoliers du Canada admissibles à recevoir leur instruction en français ou en anglais (Quebec City: Conseil de la langue française 1991), Table II.1

TABLE 6
Number and proportion of students enrolled in English-language schools in Quebec and in French-language schools outside Quebec, 1970–1 to 1988–9

School year	English in Quebec	French outside Quebec		
		NB	Ontario	Elsewhere
1970–1	248,855 (15.7%)	60,679 (34.5%)	115,869 (5.7%)	19,539 (1.0%)
1976–7	221,237 (16.8%)	53,813 (32.9%)	106,099 (5.4%)	16,194 (0.9%)
1982–3	137,678 (12.8%)	48,194 (32.6%)	93,995 (5.3%)	14,116 (0.8%)
1988–9	106,271 (10.3%)	45,308 (33.2%)	94,302 (5.1%)	14,674 (0.9%)

Sources: Statistics Canada, *Minority and Second Language Education, Elementary and Secondary Levels* Catalogue no. 81-257 (annual): 1988–9 data from 1990 edition, Table 3; earlier data from 1988 edition, Table 8
Note: The percentages shown are those obtained by dividing total enrolment in the province's schools into the enrolment in minority-language schools (the latter do not include immersion classes in majority-language schools).

schools could find themselves swamped with students who prefer to speak English. Of no less importance, the school-boards risk being controlled by parents who are not devoted francophones. However, only time will tell whether either of these possibilities actually materializes.

During the school year 1988–9 (the latest for which data are available at time of writing), there were 4.7 million students enrolled in the publicly funded schools of Canada. The historical record of minority-language school enrolment is shown in table 6. As can be seen from the table, the numbers enrolled in Quebec's English-language schools have dropped from 249,000 in 1970–1 to only 106,000 in the most recent year as Bill 101 (Chapter VIII) added its effect to those of out-migration and falling birth rates. Meanwhile, enrolment in French-language schools outside Quebec dropped from 196,000 to 154,000, despite the increasing availability of such schools.

Enrolment Eligibility
How many children are eligible to attend minority-language schools? Despite the importance of this question, no answer is available.

TABLE 7

Number and proportion of children of English mother tongue in Quebec and of French mother tongue outside Quebec, censuses of 1951, 1971 and 1986

Census year	English in Quebec	French outside Quebec		
		NB	Ontario	Elsewhere
1951	148,720	76,549	104,834	51,717
	(10.9%)	(41.6%)	(8.5%)	(3.5%)
1971	220,085	71,735	130,435	48,825
	(12.3%)	(35.3%)	(5.9%)	(2.2%)
1986	127,022	53,723	81,226	26,200
	(9.5%)	(33.3%)	(4.3%)	(1.3%)

Note: The numbers shown are of children aged 0 to 14 at the census. The percentages shown are those obtained by dividing the total number of children in the province into the number of those who are of the minority mother tongue.

It is possible to obtain, as Michel Paillé did, a special compilation of census data that will show the number of children of school age who have one or both parents of the minority mother tongue (a piece of information, incidentally, that is of no relevance when calculating potential enrolment in Quebec, since 'mother tongue' is not a criterion for admission to the minority-language schools of that province).

However, it is not possible to obtain the number of school-aged persons with at least one parent who can claim Canadian citizenship and who had received his or her education in the minority language in Canada. It is quite impossible to obtain the number of potential students who are eligible under subsection 23(2) of the charter or by virtue of provincial legislation, such as subsection 11(3) of Ontario's Bill 109.

Table 7 shows the number of children, aged 0 to 14, of English mother tongue in Quebec and of French mother tongue outside Quebec. These numbers are not intended to show potential enrolment for the minority-language schools, particularly since there are only twelve to fourteen years of schooling (including kindergarten) in the various provinces. The historical series does, however, point out the fact that there has been a sharp decline in the number of children of French mother tongue outside Quebec and an even greater drop in the number of children of English mother tongue inside Quebec, during the period between 1971 and 1986.

Federal Encouragement of Minority-Language Schools
The provinces have exclusive responsibility for primary and secondary education. However, the federal government can and does encourage schools in the minority languages. Such encouragement has since 1970, been undertaken by the secretary of state's department. One billion dollars was disbursed under the department's two relevant programs during the five-year period 1983 to 1988, and the amount will rise to $1.4 billion over the subsequent five years.[7]

The Provincial Scene
Most of Canada's minority-language children are living in three provinces: New Brunswick, Quebec, and Ontario. Selected recent happenings in these three provinces are discussed below.

Quebec
Section 93 of the British North America Act has never been repealed and is still law in Quebec. In consequence, there are English-language schools in that province that are administered by the predominantly French 'Catholic' boards as well as French-language schools under the usually English 'Protestant' (actually, non-Catholic) boards.

In 1984, the government of René Lévesque passed Bill 3, which provided for division of the province's schools by language rather than by religion. However, the Quebec Association of Protestant School Boards applied to the courts to have the law declared unconstitutional. Their action would appear to have been motivated by mistrust; since the great majority of non-Catholics are English-speaking, the existing division of schools along religious lines has provided, in practice, a constitutional guarantee for the continuing existence of an English-language school system.

Bill 3 was struck down by the Quebec Superior Court; the judgment was not appealed, as the Péquiste government was defeated in the general elections of 1985. The new minister of education, Claude Ryan, introduced a new piece of legislation (Bill 107) that may have avoided the technical defects of its predecessor. Although the new bill has passed the scrutiny of lower courts, it will probably be taken to the Supreme Court of Canada for a final decision.

---

7 *Language and Society* 24 (Fall 1988), 35. The programs are Official Languages in Education and Promotion of Official Languages.

Meanwhile, chapter VIII of Bill 101 is being rigorously applied, and the number of pupils enrolled in English-language schools has dropped sharply (this law obliges the children of almost all immigrants, even those from the United Kingdom, to attend French-language primary and secondary schools).

Ontario

Although a French-language school-board for Ottawa had been originally proposed by the pastor of St Patrick's Church,[8] the legislation was not introduced until seventy years later. On 12 December 1985, Premier David Peterson announced that Ontario's first such board would be established in the nation's capital. The enabling legislation, Bill 109, was given first reading in April 1988 and received Royal Assent in time for the school elections held in the fall of that year.

Ottawa-Carleton is the logical location for such a board, since one-quarter of the province's francophones live within this regional municipality. Almost 85,000 persons chose to support the French-language board at the enumeration of 1988; although this number fell well short of the 125,000 hoped for by promoters of the board, it must be remembered that anyone who failed to register as a French-language elector was included in the English-language public-school or separate-school rolls.

To counter possible court challenges under section 93 of the British North America Act, Bill 109 provided for two sectors, the schools being divided along religious lines. The new board began functioning on 1 January 1989, taking over some fifty French-language schools, and their pupils, that had formerly been administered by the four older boards of the municipality. The board began, therefore, with approximately 12,500 students at the elementary level and 5,600 at the secondary level.

Constitutional questions aside, the main problem faced by the new board is financial. If the tax rates for the French-language board are higher than those for the existing boards, many eligible ratepayers will be discouraged from switching their support. The alternative to higher local taxes is massive subsidization by the province; initially, provincial funding was freely given, but the future is not clear.

---

8 *Ottawa Journal*, 13 February 1915

New Brunswick

Because New Brunswick was not mentioned in section 93 of the British North America Act, it has been free to organize its schools along language lines, and all schools are, at least in theory, non-sectarian.

The province took over schools from local boards in 1966 to provide more equal funding in the poorer districts. Since the early 1980s, schools have been devoted to one or the other of the two official languages; each part of the province may have two school-boards, one responsible for all the French-language schools in the district and the other for all the English-language schools in an overlapping but not necessarily identical district.

Within the Department of Education, the division between French and English goes all the way to the top, with two deputy ministers, one for each language group, reporting to the minister. However, instruction in a second language has been included in the list of compulsory subjects, with emphasis on oral skills.

School-board elections are held every three years. In 1986, there was no preliminary identification of voters by language, and each person entering a voting station was free to vote for members of either the French or the English board. The Department of Education recognized the potential problems inherent in this informality; the Schools Act was amended and now provides that, at the enumeration preceding the 1989 and subsequent elections, each voter must declare for which board he or she wishes to vote.

11

The United States

Although this book is concerned with the status of the French language in Canada, the situation in the United States cannot be ignored. If Canada were located beside a country in which most of the people spoke French, then it would not be that language that was threatened. One of the factors putting pressure on the French language in Canada is the overwhelming influence of English in almost everything emanating from the United States.

Maps can be deceptive. A map of North America, as it was about the year 1700, shows a relatively small English-speaking area along the Atlantic seaboard, with a vast expanse of French blue stretching from Acadia up the St Lawrence to the prairies and down the Mississippi to New Orleans. However, territory and population are not the same. When a census of the new colonies was taken in 1765, there were only 70,000 French Canadians plus about 10,000 Acadians; in contrast, the total population approached two million in the older British colonies of North America.

This chapter will look chiefly at the Franco-Americans, the descendants of persons who migrated south from Canada during the nineteenth and twentieth centuries. Generally ignored will be the 'Cajuns' of Louisiana; although not negligible in numbers, they have had very little influence on the language situation in Canada, particularly since the recent death of James Domengeaux, former guiding force of the Conseil pour le développement du français en Louisiane (CODOFIL).

When the Thirteen Colonies won their independence from the British crown, their language remained English. Immigrants arriving during the next two centuries took it for granted that they had to speak the language of the majority; if they could not speak English on arrival, they (and their children) rapidly became anglophones.

This anglicization of immigrant families affected not only newcomers from Europe but also the many thousands of French-speaking Canadians who had migrated to the mill towns of New England and to other destinations in the United States. Although the immigrants themselves and (usually) their children retained the French language, the third and fourth generations tended to assimilate into the majority language of their country of birth.[1]

The U.S. census of 1900 reported 1,179,807 persons who had been born in Canada; this number would, of course, not include any immigrants who had died before 1900, had moved on to some other country, or had returned to Canada. Also missing from this total were the many persons who had been born in Europe or elsewhere and had lived in Canada before migrating to the United States.

For statistical purposes, the U.S. authorities distinguished two categories of Canadian-born persons moving south. Approximately one-third of these spoke French and were reported separately.

At the turn of the century, there were 395,000 French-Canadian immigrants living in the United States, plus 456,000 native-born children of French Canadians; 61 per cent of these latter were of two Canadian-born parents and the remainder had one U.S.-born parent.

According to our own census of 1901, there were 1,649,371 persons of French origin living in Canada. Noting that many persons of French origin would not have been reported by the U.S. census because both their parents were 'native-born,' it can be seen that the southward migration of the nineteenth century had very seriously reduced the French-origin population of Canada.

Today, there are perhaps two million people in New England who might be called Franco-Americans. However, a recent newspaper article states that many of these, including even some of the leaders of Franco-American organizations, are unilingual anglophones who happen to be of Quebec or Acadian descent.[2] In other words, they are what Serge Joyal, when secretary of state, referred to as 'Francogènes': people who have some degree of attachment to the French culture of their ancestors but who do not speak the French language.

1 This point was discussed in my *Languages in Conflict* (Montreal 1967), 71–2.
2 George Tombs, 'Franco-Americans grapple with assimilation,' the *Gazette* (Montreal), 13 August 1988, B5

An assessment of the present strength of the French language south of the border is hampered by the fact that the U.S. census is quite different from that to which we are accustomed in Canada. The questions are different, the instructions are different, and the editing procedures are different, to reflect the quite different objectives of the two censuses.

The Canadian censuses have asked three questions on language, including one (mother tongue) that is asked of all Canadians. In contrast, the U.S. census puts the emphasis on ethnicity and relegates its one language question to the long form that is sent to only a sample of the population. The language question of the 1980 U.S. census asked:

13a. Does this person speak a language other than English at home?
  b. What is this language?
  c. How well does the person speak *English*?

A survey made in 1979 showed that 76 per cent of all those who reported French as a language currently spoken in their homes had stated that they spoke English 'very well' and that an additional 18 per cent claimed to speak it 'well'; less than 6 per cent spoke the majority language 'not well' or 'not at all.' There is a strong suggestion that many of those reporting French would be, by Canadian standards, of English home language. In other words, the U.S. question exaggerates the number of those speaking languages other than English.

Although there are obvious problems in interpreting the census data, it seems safe to say that, of the 227 million persons living in the fifty states in 1980, at least 200 million were anglos, in the Canadian sense of the word. This figure is derived after deducting 14 million for Spanish-speakers, one million or so for French-speakers, and a few millions for those who were most at home in some other language.

The low degree of importance attached to the French language in the United States is underlined by the fact that every census questionnaire distributed in 1980 had a note on the cover, written in Spanish, advising the recipient that forms were available in Spanish and might be obtained by simply returning the (otherwise blank) English-language questionnaire, after checking a box asking for the

Spanish version. There was no similar note in French or in any other language.

Incidentally, the lobbying power of the Hispanic groups in the United States has been such that the printing of 1970 census forms was halted so that an additional question could be added for the better identification of Hispanics. The questionnaires sent out in 1980 were drawn up only after long and sometimes acrimonious discussions between representatives of the Census Bureau and of the Hispanics.[3] No francophone organization in the United States can exert comparable influence.

A recent publication of Quebec's Conseil de la langue française concludes that 'by the end of the century, the Franco-American community will include only a quarter of a million persons for whom French is a daily language; of these, three-quarters will not have been born in the United States ... Native-born or immigrants, we will be looking at a language group that is in steep decline, since it will include many older persons.'[4] Meanwhile, of course, the overwhelmingly English nature of the United States is having its effects on this side of the border. Many Canadians can watch U.S. television shows in their original language; even those who restrict themselves to the French-language channels often receive translated programs that convey U.S. values to formerly isolated francophone communities (it will be ironic if René Lévesque goes down in history as the person who, perhaps more than any other, popularized television among French-speaking Canadians and, thereby, played an important part in their demographic decline).

3 Harvey M. Choldin, 'Statistics and Politics: The "Hispanic Issue" in the 1980 Census,' *Demography*, August 1986, 407, 410ff
4 Calvin Veltman, *L'avenir du français aux Etats-Unis*, no. 27 in the series Documentation du Conseil de la langue française (Quebec City 1987), 225

12

The Atlantic Region

With the exception of the seven northern counties of New Brunswick, which must be examined as a separate region, Canada's four Atlantic provinces are overwhelmingly English-speaking. This situation is, in large part, attributable to the fact that the great majority of their inhabitants are of British origins, descendants of either direct immigrants from the British Isles or Loyalists who came north from the United States.

Atlantic Canada is the northern limit of colonization along the east coast of North America. Spain and Portugal, so active south of Georgia, did not attempt to settle this area, if we disregard the sixteenth-century Basque whaling establishments in Labrador. Sweden and Holland did found colonies along the Delaware and Hudson rivers, but these had passed to British control by 1664.

Until 1763, France and Britain fought over what is now Canada. France was, initially, in control of Acadia and the St Lawrence, while British colonies lined the seaboard elsewhere. The frontier regions were the scene of intermittent raids by small forces of regulars or militia (Iberville had only 125 Canadiens with him when he virtually achieved the conquest of Newfoundland in 1696) but transfers of territory were usually decided by the outcome of warfare in Europe.

The Treaty of Utrecht, in 1713, marked the beginning of the end for French rule in North America, as France gave back to Britain the posts it had captured on Hudson Bay and also ceded Newfoundland and what was loosely described as 'Acadia,' the mainland portion of today's Nova Scotia.

In 1745, the newly built fortress of Louisbourg surrendered to a force composed largely of New Englanders, escorted by ships of the

Royal Navy. When Cape Breton was returned to France in 1748, several thousand British settlers were established at Halifax, to counterbalance this restored French presence.

In 1750, French forces under Le Loutre forced many Acadians to leave their homes around Beaubassin and to move to the French side of Forts Beauséjour and Gaspereau, located on what is now the border between Nova Scotia and New Brunswick. Five years later, about six thousand Acadians were deported from their homes at Port Royal and elsewhere in Nova Scotia, after they had refused to take the required oath of allegiance to the British crown.

Later in 1755, British and New England troops took the two French forts. In 1758, Louisbourg was again captured and became the springboard for British operations against the French colony along the St Lawrence. By 1760, British forces were in complete control of what are now the Atlantic provinces of Canada.

By the Treaty of Paris, signed in 1763, the King of France renounced all his pretensions to Canada, including the Acadian area, with the exception of the islands of St Pierre and Miquelon. The former lands of the Acadians could then be given to English-speaking settlers, including the Loyalists who came north after 1783. Many of the Acadians who returned from exile were obliged to seek new lands in the north of New Brunswick.

Later immigrants to Canada seldom settled in the Atlantic provinces, and the growth of this region was inhibited by net out-migration, as many of its young people went to the United States or to other parts of Canada. In 1986, only 9 per cent of Canada's population were living in the four easternmost provinces.

As noted at the opening of this chapter, most of the French-speaking residents of the Atlantic area are to be found in the north of New Brunswick. Elsewhere, in the provinces of Newfoundland, Prince Edward Island, and Nova Scotia, and in the southern half of New Brunswick, barely more than 2 per cent of the population reported to the 1986 census that French was the language they spoke most often in their own homes.

Table 8 shows the historical record of the French-speaking population of the three easternmost provinces. In Prince Edward Island and Nova Scotia (data are not available for Newfoundland prior to 1949), the proportion of the population reporting French ethnic origin may actually have increased slightly between 1911 and 1951, so it would appear, from the sharply declining language figures, that an-

TABLE 8
'French' population of the three easternmost provinces, in actual numbers and as a proportion of the total population, censuses of 1911, 1951, and 1986

Province	1911 EO[a]	1951 EO	1951 MT[b]	1986 MT	1986 HL[c]
Nova Scotia	51,746	73,760	38,945	35,810	24,720
	(10.5%)	(11.5%)	(6.1%)	(4.1%)	(2.9%)
PEI	13,117	15,477	8,477	5,920	3,485
	(14.0%)	(15.7%)	(8.6%)	(4.7%)	(2.8%)
Newfoundland	n/a[d]	9,841	2,321	2,670	2,110
	n/a	(2.7%)	(0.6%)	(0.5%)	(0.4%)

[a] EO = 'by ethnic origin': by 1986, 'ethnic origin' had so changed in definition that the numbers cannot be compared with those for earlier years.
[b] MT = 'by mother tongue': 'mother tongue' was not asked in 1911.
[c] HL = 'by home language': 'home language' was not asked in 1911 or 1951.
[d] Newfoundland was not included in the 1911 census of Canada.

glicization has been very active in this region (ethnic origin had so changed in definition by 1986 that the data of that census are not comparable with those of 1911 and 1951, and are not shown).

Comments on Nova Scotia, Prince Edward Island, and Newfoundland follow; New Brunswick (the entire province, not just the seven northern counties) is the subject of a separate chapter.

Nova Scotia and Prince Edward Island
The 1911 census showed that 10.5 per cent of the population of Nova Scotia was of French origin, as was 14 per cent of that of Prince Edward Island. In 1986, after distributing the many multiple responses, it would appear that the proportions had changed only slightly during the intervening seventy-five years. (It is not possible to make a more precise statement, since the 'ethnic origin' criteria changed substantially between 1911 and 1986.)

However, as table 8 shows, only 2.9 per cent and 2.8 per cent, respectively, of the populations of the two provinces reported French as the language they were speaking most often in their own homes in 1986. Anglicization would appear to have been heavy in both provinces.

Those who still speak French are to be found mainly in rural areas, notably Yarmouth and Digby counties of mainland Nova Scotia, Richmond and Inverness Counties of Cape Breton Island, and the western part of Prince Edward Island. In the metropolitan area of Halifax, with a total population of 296,000, only 3,110 persons gave the single response 'French' to the 'home language' question of the 1986 census.

The future of the French language in these two provinces does not seem promising, particularly since even the Acadians are divided as to the language in which they wish their children to be educated. There was a well-publicized instance of this in 1985, when the population of Cheticamp, in Inverness County, defeated, by a margin of almost two to one, a proposal that the town's only school should teach a curriculum emphasizing the French language.

Newfoundland

Some special problems must be faced when handling data from Newfoundland, since Newfoundland joined Confederation in 1949 and neither ethnic origin nor mother tongue was asked at censuses prior to that of 1951. Also, the data for Newfoundland and Labrador are not included in data for Canada as of any earlier year.

In 1951, there were 9,841 persons of French origin in Newfoundland but only 2,321 of French mother tongue; the latter figure is barely more than 0.5 per cent of the total population of 361,416. More than three-quarters of those claiming French as the mother tongue were found in an area along the south end of the island's west coast, just west of Stephenville; this was the only part of the island recommended as a bilingual district by the second board (in 1975). However, the number (not just the proportion) of francophones in this area has been dropping and is now down to only a few hundred.

Labrador seemed to be the next hub of Newfoundland's French-speaking population, as workers came in from Quebec to work in the iron mines. However, after reaching a peak in 1971, the number of francophones has declined, and they represent only about 2 per cent of the present population of Labrador.

In 1986, the metropolitan area of St John's had a total population of 162,000 but only about 500 were francophones, and the importance of the French language is far less here than it is in Halifax or the cities of New Brunswick.

It is possible that the announcement of an offshore oil project will attract job-seekers from Quebec and cause a jump in the number of francophones in Newfoundland. However, unless there is net in-migration of French-speakers, the minority-language population of this province seems destined to continue its decline.

13

New Brunswick

On 8 July 1760, British ships forced their way up the Restigouche River, at the west end of the Baie des Chaleurs, and destroyed a small fleet that had been sent from France to assist the hard-pressed French army in Canada. The Battle of the Restigouche, as it is called, came two years after the capture of Louisbourg and ended formal French resistance in the Acadian area.

By the Treaty of Paris, signed in 1763, France renounced all pretensions to Acadia. This included Cape Breton Island and Ile-Saint-Jean (now Prince Edward Island) as well as the mainland, today's Nova Scotia and New Brunswick. In 1765, after the return to France of those who did not wish to remain in what had become British territory, the estimated French-origin population of the Acadian areas was just over 10,000 persons.

This population was augmented by the return of some of those who had been banished from Nova Scotia during the recent war, after they had refused to take the required oath of allegiance to the British crown. As their lands in Nova Scotia and southern New Brunswick had been occupied by Loyalists forced out of the American colonies after 1783, most of those returning had to find new lands in the north and east of New Brunswick.

The area near the headwaters of the Saint John River was also occupied by colonists of French origin, but the region was long disputed by Quebec and New Brunswick. In 1851, London awarded to New Brunswick what is today the northwest corner of the province (Madawaska County and the adjoining municipalities of Victoria and Restigouche counties).[1]

1 Statutes of the United Kingdom, 14–15 Victoria, 1851

Growing from these three origins, New Brunswick's French population in 1871 was 44,907 persons in a total population of 285,594 (16 per cent). Nearly all of these were in the north and east of the province, with French majorities in the counties of Gloucester, Kent, and Victoria (which then included what is today Madawaska) and with a sizeable French community in Westmorland County, chiefly to the east of where Moncton stands today.

Between 1871 and 1921, the French population of New Brunswick grew at an impressive rate, while the non-French population was seriously weakened by emigration, chiefly to New England. Over the fifty-year period, the non-French population increased by less than 11 per cent, while the French population increased by 170 per cent. By 1910, a well-informed outsider, looking at this great discrepancy in growth rates, wrote: 'Before 20 more years have passed, they [the Acadians] will constitute the absolute majority of the population of New Brunswick.'[2] At the 1911 census, taken less than a year after these words had been written, 28 per cent of the province's total population was of French origin, and Henri Bourassa's prediction did not seem unreasonable.

Ten years later, just over 31 per cent of New Brunswick's population was of French origin, and the proportion rose to 33.6 per cent in 1931. However, a slow-down in the rate of increase of the French population and a notable improvement in the net rate of increase of the non-French population combined to frustrate all possibility of a French majority in New Brunswick.

By 1961, the census at which their relative strength reached its peak, persons of French origin made up just under 39 per cent of the total population, well short of a majority, and their relative strength dropped to 37 per cent at the census taken in 1971.

In addition, by 1971, it had become evident that the 'ethnic origin' data were overstating the importance of the French-speaking minority and that there was a widening gap between the number of people who were of French origin (the numbers given in this chapter so far) and the number who were still speaking French.

From the 'mother tongue' question of the census, introduced in 1931, it could be seen that the relative strength of the French-speaking population had peaked in 1951, at 35.9 per cent. The trend since that date has been downwards, to 35.2 per cent in 1961 and (using the

2 Henri Bourassa, in *Le Devoir*, 7 August 1910, 1

adjusted data published by Statistics Canada) to 33.5 per cent in 1986. It will be noted that the latter proportion is back down to the level of the mid-1930s.

The most recent language question of the census, that on the language spoken at home, gives an even lower proportion. By this criterion, only 31.3 per cent of New Brunswick's 1986 population could be described as francophone, even after counting in almost half the 22,355 persons who reported that they spoke both English and French in their homes (see tables 27 and 28).

The numbers cited above are for the population of all ages. The breakdown by age groups shows that there has been a considerable drop in French birth rates. At present, about 3,300 babies born each year are of French mother tongue; in the early 1950s, more than 6,000 babies of French mother tongue were being born each year, although there had been considerably fewer French-speaking women of child-bearing age.

Although non-French births have also been declining in number, the rate of decline has not been as great. In consequence, the rate of birth among non-French families is now about equal to that of the French. In 1986, only 32.9 per cent of the 0–4 age group were of French mother tongue, compared to 41.3 per cent in 1951 and 42.3 per cent in 1941. This finding shows that there is no longer a higher rate of natural increase among the francophones to compensate for the losses that their group is suffering through anglicization.

It was noted previously that the French-speaking settlements had been located in the northwest, the northeast, and the east of the province. This situation has continued down to the present day, with very few francophones living in the southern eight counties, as can be seen from table 9, based on the 'home language' data of the census taken in 1986.

The distribution of the francophone population of New Brunswick has taken on considerable significance with the decline of the traditional rural industries, since there is now a drift into the cities, where English is usually the predominant language.

Saint John, on the Bay of Fundy, had a population of 121,265 within its metropolitan area. Of these, only 2,445 reported French as the language they were using in their own homes (1986 census data). The provincial capital, Fredericton, showed 11,100 people who claimed to be able to converse in French, but only 2,205 of these reported

TABLE 9

Total population and proportion giving the single response 'English' or 'French' to the 'home language' question of the 1986 census, three areas of New Brunswick

Area	Total population	English (%)	French (%)
North[a]	300,764	35	59
Moncton[b]	102,081	70	24
South[c]	306,595	96[d]	2

[a] The seven northern counties, less that part of Westmorland within the Moncton census area
[b] The census agglomeration of Moncton
[c] The eight southern counties, less that part of Albert within the Moncton census area
[d] The proportions do not add up to 100 per cent because the figures for multiple replies and for non-official languages are not shown.

French as their home language, in a total population of 65,765. The 1986 census data for Moncton are shown in table 9.

Even in the extreme north of the province, along the Baie des Chaleurs, francophones are to be found chiefly in rural areas, while anglos are concentrated in the cities and towns. The one notable exception to this general rule is Edmundston, where over 90 per cent of the citizens are francophones.

Disregarding this rural/urban split and looking only at the fact that French is the majority language in the seven northern counties, the suggestion has been made that these counties should be detached from New Brunswick and made into a new province.[3] The north has about 54 per cent of the total population of New Brunswick but about 95 per cent of its francophones; in the eight counties of the south, the 1986 population of 328,435 included fewer than 10,000 persons of French home language.

However, a simple separation of the seven northern counties seems out of the question. Moncton, the only major city in the area, is overwhelmingly English-speaking, as is Northumberland County; Victoria County also has a substantial English-speaking majority. It is unlikely that the people of these three areas would vote to place themselves under the control of a French-dominated legislature.

3 'Les Acadiens ressuscitent le projet d'une province,' Le Devoir, 2 June 1986, 4

One alternative would be to split off only about two-thirds of the north, dividing counties along municipal boundaries in many cases (e.g., the three northernmost municipalities of Victoria County are overwhelmingly French and would go to the new province, while the remainder of the county, with its chiefly English-speaking population, would remain part of New Brunswick). The result would be an eleventh province with a total population of about 240,000, of which some 80 per cent would be francophones.

Several practical difficulties tend to inhibit the adoption of this proposal, including:

- the area to be split off from New Brunswick stretches along the north and east sides of the present province, with Kent County and the French-speaking part of Westmorland County separated from Gloucester and the other northern counties;
- the area is predominantly rural; Edmundston (population 11,497) is the largest city with a predominantly francophone population (Bathurst is larger than Edmundston but is not a francophone city); and
- the 45,000 anglos who would be obliged to live in the new province can be expected to protest their proposed minority status.

It might be feasible to split off the overwhelmingly French northwest (Madawaska County plus contiguous areas of Victoria and Restigouche). However, the total population would be only 52,000, so this corner would probably become part of Quebec (ironically, reversing the judgment rendered by London in 1851!), rather than a separate province. The result would tend to be a weakening of the status of the Acadians living elsewhere in New Brunswick.

To counter the pull of Quebec, or of an Acadian province, successive provincial governments in recent years have tried to hold New Brunswick together by passing legislation that improves the status of the French-speaking minority. In 1969, the Liberal government of Premier (now Senator) Louis Robichaud passed the Official Languages Act. This legislation was based on the federal act of the same name and included the following statement:

the English and French languages
a) are the official languages of New Brunswick ... and
b) possess and enjoy equality of status ...

TABLE 10

Province of New Brunswick, total population and 'French' population, censuses of 1871 to 1986 (adjusted data)

Census	Total population	'French' population	French/ Total (%)
1871 EO[a]	285,594	44,907	15.7
1901 EO	331,120	79,979	24.2
1931 EO	408,219	136,999	33.6
1951 EO	515,697	197,631	38.3
MT[b]	515,697	185,110	35.9
1961 EO	597,936	232,127	38.8
MT	597,936	210,530	35.2
1971 EO	634,560	235,025	37.0
MT	634,560	215,725	34.0
HL[c]	634,560	199,080	31.4
1986 MT	709,445[d]	237,570	33.5
HL	701,885[e]	219,350[f]	31.3

[a] EO = 'by ethnic origin.'
[b] MT = 'by mother tongue.'
[c] HL = 'by home language.'
[d] The total population shown in 1986 did not include an estimated 980 persons living on non-cooperating Indian reserves.
[e] The number used when calculating the proportion of persons of French home language excludes inmates of institutions as well as persons living on non-cooperating Indian reserves.
[f] The 'French' population in 1986 included 208,545 persons (29.7 per cent of the total population) who replied 'French' to the census question on home language; the figure shown is as published by Statistics Canada after allocation of all multiple responses.

In 1981, the Conservative government of Premier Richard Hatfield passed further legislation. The purpose of this legislation is indicated by its name: 'An Act concerning the Equality of the Two Official Language Communities.' In 1982, the Constitution Act (debated by Parliament in 1981) named New Brunswick as a bilingual province and provided that, inter alia, 'any member of the public in New Brunswick has the right to communicate with, and to receive available services from, any office of an institution of the legislature or government of New Brunswick in English or French.'

Despite these laws, there has still been considerable discontent on the part of Acadians who felt that their language group was not being treated as well as was the English-speaking majority. Much valuable information on the situation in New Brunswick can be obtained from the report of the Task Force on Official Languages, presented to the premier on 31 March 1982.[4] It should be noted, however, that the government chose not to act on most of the recommendations of the report, although it did provide parallel school-boards, one set for English-speaking students and the other for French-speakers.

The future of the French language in New Brunswick is not clear. As table 10 shows, the relative numerical strength of the French majority peaked in 1951 or 1961, depending on the criterion used, and has now fallen back to the level of the 1930s. One well-informed Acadian has called attention to the ageing of the French-speaking population and has gone on record as stating that the language is in greater danger than it was some ten years earlier.[5]

4 Cabinet Secretariat, Official Languages Branch, *Towards Equality of the Official Languages in New Brunswick* (Fredericton 1982)
5 Michel Bastarache, in *Demolinguistic Trends and the Evolution of Canadian Institutions* (Montreal: Association for Canadian Studies, Department of the Secretary of State, and Office of the Commissioner for Official Languages 1989), 185

14

Quebec: The Province

Cod fishermen from Brittany were familiar with the Gulf of St Lawrence by the early part of the sixteenth century, and Jacques Cartier made several voyages of exploration from 1534 on. However, it was not until 1600 that, impelled by the increasing demand for North American pelts, the French established a trading post at Tadoussac.

In 1608, Champlain built his Habitation on the present site of Quebec City. The colony was captured by the brothers Kirke in 1629 but was bought back by France in 1632. Montreal was founded in 1642 as a link to the Great Lakes. Colonists were established along the St Lawrence from Montreal down to well past Quebec City, and women were sent out from France to promote natural increase, but not until about 1680 did the population of the colony reached the 10,000 level. This slow growth was due, chiefly, to the reluctance of potential immigrants to leave France for a life in a land that was covered in snow for half the year.

By 1713, the year during which the Treaty of Utrecht marked the beginning of the end of French rule in North America, the population of Canada had reached a mere 18,469 persons, excluding Indians. A census taken in 1765, two years after the Treaty of Paris, counted only 70,000 persons of French origin; in contrast, there were almost two million inhabitants in the other British colonies of North America.

During the French regime, the colony along the St Lawrence had been known as 'La Nouvelle France' or 'Le Canada' (the term 'Le Gouvernement de Québec' referred to an administrative region around Quebec City, bounded on the west by 'Le Gouvernement des Trois-Rivières'). The 'Province of Quebec' was established in 1763 by Royal Proclamation, and originally stretched from the Gaspé Peninsula westward into the future union. In 1783, the southwest was lost, including Detroit and Niagara. In 1791, Ontario (as it is called today) was split off from Quebec. Ungava was added to the province in 1912, and the Labrador boundary was resolved in 1927, but, for all practical purposes, historical studies of the size and characteristics of Quebec's population can go back to 1791.

An estimate of the population of Lower Canada in 1837 states that there were 166,000 'English' (sic) and 434,000 'French'; in other words, approximately 28 per cent of the inhabitants of Lower Canada were then English-speaking. This proportion reflects substantial immigration from both the British Isles and the United States; the strength of this immigration misled Lord Durham's advisers into forecasting that the French language in North America would inevitably be submerged.

Despite the arrival of tens of thousands of Irish, fleeing the hunger and poverty of their native land, the proportion of persons of French origin rose at each successive census, as many of the non-French turned their backs on Quebec and headed for the better prospects they could envisage elsewhere.[1] By 1861, the census prior to Confederation, the total population of the province had risen to 1.11 million, but the non-French were down to less than 24 per cent of the total.

Between 1861 and 1901, there was heavy southward emigration, which slowed the rate of growth of Quebec's population but particularly affected those who were of non-French origins. By 1901, Quebec's population had increased to 1,648,898, with 80.2 per cent of these being of French origin. Persons of Irish origin (7 per cent) were still in second place, ahead of those of English, Scottish, and other British origins.

Substantial net immigration occurred during the first decade of the present century, with many newcomers arriving from eastern and southern Europe. By 1911, the number of persons of Jewish origin in Quebec exceeded 30,000, which became the most important group of non-French, non-British origin. However, there had been a disappearance of many persons of Irish origin. In consequence, the 1.6 million persons of French origin in the province in 1911 represented 80.1 per cent of the total population, a proportion virtually unchanged from the previous high reached in 1901.

---

1 Raoul Blanchard refers to 'L'invasion irlandaise' in Le Canada français (Montreal: Librairie Arthème Fayard 1960), 77–8.

The quantitative strength of the French-origin group was accompanied by an increase in their qualitative strength. In 1910, the legislature passed La Loi Lavergne, which required all public utility companies in Quebec to print their documents in French as well as in English; for train and tram companies, 'documents' included their tickets (mild as this requirement may seem today, the measure passed the Bills Committee of the Legislative Council [the upper house] by only a four-vote margin). In the fall of the same year, L'École des Hautes Études Commerciales opened its doors, to promote a French presence in the world of commerce.

Reflecting continued heavy immigration, the French proportion of Quebec's population slipped slightly, to 79 per cent, in 1931. However, immigration virtually ceased during the depression era, and the 1951 census showed 82.0 per cent of Quebec's population as being of French origin, 82.5 per cent of French mother tongue.

Heavy postwar immigration then began to adversely affect the relative strength of the French population. The 1971 census reported that only 80.7 per cent of Quebec residents gave French as their mother tongue (80.8 per cent were of French home language). At that census, there were 468,925 foreign-born persons in Quebec and an additional 256,260 who had been born in Canada, but outside Quebec.

Two aspects of the 1971 census results must be noted. There had been a dip in the proportion of francophones among Quebec's population, wiping out the slow gains of many decades. Equally significant was the related fact that most immigrants had obviously not integrated to the French-speaking community, since the number of persons of French home language (4,870,105) was barely higher than the number who were of French mother tongue (4,867,250).

Quebec's 'nationalists' seized upon the results of the 1971 census as justification for Bill 22 (in 1974) and Bill 101 (passed in 1977). Both these pieces of legislation declared French to be the only language of Quebec,[2] and Bill 101, in particular, severely restricted the number of children who would be permitted to attend English-language schools, as well as regulating the language of work, of public signs, etc.

Several provisions of Bill 101 have been appealed to the courts,

2 The first section of Bill 101 reads: 'French is the official language of Québec [sic].'

usually (but not always) with success. These court cases have led to a broadening of the categories of persons who may send their children to Quebec's English-language schools; such persons now include all Canadian citizens who have received their elementary instruction in English anywhere in Canada (the 'Canada clause'). However, the Supreme Court's ruling on the language of signs was circumvented by Premier Bourassa's use of the 'notwithstanding clause' in Bill 178.

The election of a Péquiste government in 1976 and the subsequent introduction of La Charte de la langue française (Bill 101) were followed by an exodus from Quebec; according to data published by the Bureau de la statistique du Québec, just over 323,000 persons moved out of the province during the five years from 1976 to 1981 and a further 234,000 moved out in 1981–6.[3]

The consequences of all these events can be seen in table 11, which shows the 'English' population of Quebec. Although a cause-and-effect relationship between these events may be difficult to prove, it is a fact that this outward movement affected chiefly the English-speaking minority of the province's population. As noted in chapter 8, analysis of the data from the 1981 census showed that francophones made up fewer than one-fifth of persons reported as having moved from Quebec to another part of Canada during the period from 1976 to 1981.

A significant factor to note was that the departure of Quebec's anglos particularly affected the young adults. To illustrate, the 1971 census showed 111,000 women aged 10 to 24 who were of English mother tongue; in 1986, however, there were only 81,000 women of English mother tongue aged 25 to 39 in Quebec, even though there must have been both immigration and in-migration during the intervening fifteen years. The conclusion seems to be that over one-quarter of this group left the province; if they had children, these would be counted elsewhere.

(In contrast, it might be noted, net migration during the same fifteen years had not significantly affected the number of young adult females of French mother tongue in Ontario. Those aged 25 to 39 in 1986 were almost as numerous as the 68,000 aged 10 to 24 in 1971.)

Obviously, the departure of so many of its former (and of its potential) residents has had a negative effect on Quebec's growth. Cur-

---

3 Bureau de la statistique du Québec, *La situation démographique au Québec*, 1990 edition (Quebec City 1991), Table 601

TABLE 11
Province of Quebec, total population and 'English' population, censuses of 1871 to 1986 (adjusted data)

Census	Total population	'English' population	'English'/ total (%)
1871 BO[a]	1,192[d]	243	20.4
1901 BO	1,649	290	17.6
1931 BO	2,874	433	15.1
1951 BO	4,056	492	12.1
EMT[b]	''	558	13.8
1971 BO	6,028	640	10.6
EMT	''	789	13.1
EHL[c]	''	888	14.7
1986 EMT	6,532	679	10.4
EHL	6,454[e]	797	12.3

a   BO = 'of British origins.'
b   EMT = 'of English mother tongue.'
c   EHL = 'of English home language.'
d   All numbers are in thousands.
e   The 1986 total population used for home language was only 6,454,495; this figure excludes inmates of institutions as well as an estimated 7,815 persons living on certain Indian reserves.
    The 'English' population in 1986 included 676,050 persons who gave the single response 'English' to the census question on home language; the figure of 796,695 is as published by Statistics Canada after allocation of all multiple responses.

rently, the province's population is less than 25.4 per cent of that of Canada; in 1951, at the first census to include Newfoundland, Quebec held almost 29 per cent of the country's population. This drop in relative population weight has been, of course, reflected in a drop in political importance.

Loss of population through migration has been only one of the factors slowing Quebec's population growth. As noted in chapter 6, the drop in Quebec's birth rate has been of even greater importance. Although 97,500 babies (preliminary figure) were born in Quebec in 1990, an increase of 17 per cent from the low of 83,600 reported for 1987, the birth rate is still less than half that averaged during the 1950s and, incidentally, is still well below the minimum required for replacement of the older generations. Quebec's age 'pyramid' looks more like a haystack with the lower levels eaten away.[4]

Quebec is, therefore, facing at least two major problems: the drop in birth rates, which affects both official language groups, and the selective out-migration of the English-speaking population.

Quebec's political leaders do not hesitate to invoke the concept of 'collective rights' when the matter under discussion is the use of English words on signs. In contrast, they hesitate to introduce legislation intended to increase family size, with the exception, of course, of the incentives described in chapter 6.

There are political dangers in any measure intended to openly encourage anglos to remain in Quebec, since the departure of persons who prefer to speak English has been the most effective way of reducing the size of the linguistic minority in the province.

Government policy that encourages francophones from the other provinces to move to Quebec has several attractive features. Most francophones elsewhere in Canada have family connections with people living in Quebec, so the newcomers would have to make only minimal cultural adjustments. However, only a government that had written off the minorities elsewhere could deliberately encourage migration that would further weaken the French-speaking communities in the other provinces.

There remains the expedient of bringing in francophones or 'francophonisables' from outside Canada. Quebec's interest in taking greater control of immigration into the province has been described in chapter 7. However, absorbing newcomers will result in a reduction in the present homogeneity of the French-speaking population of Quebec. As Senator Jacques Hébert summarized the situation: 'Québécois well know that their future ... no longer depends on "la revanche des berceaux" ... and that the Québécois of the future will have a dark skin or slanted eyes.'[5]

---

4 Ibid, 23
5 Senator Jacques Hébert, *Senate Debates*, 17 May 1988, 3397

15

Quebec: The Two Regions

As was emphasized in *Languages in Conflict*, there are two quite distinct linguistic regions within what might be called the inhabited area of Quebec province.[1]

The north and east of this area, with Quebec City as its centre, is overwhelmingly French-speaking by all criteria. English is the home language of only 3 per cent of the population of this region, and nearly all the others use French in their homes as well as in public.

The south and west of the province are quite different. At the 1986 census, English was the home language of 21 per cent of the population of Montreal, of almost 13 per cent of that of the Eastern Townships, and of 20 per cent of those living in the Ottawa Valley. Although French-speakers are clearly in the majority in each of these areas, the strength of the English language in this region is far ahead of that in the north and east of the province.

As more than four-fifths of the anglos (by home language) living in the south and west of Quebec are to be found within the census metropolitan area of Montreal, the next section of this chapter will be devoted to a brief outline of the historical development and present situation of that community; the other parts of the region will, with regret, be disregarded.

Later pages of this chapter will discuss the north and east of Quebec, the only region of Canada in which the French language is overwhelmingly dominant. Finally, the special status of the Ungava Peninsula will be noted.

1 Richard J. Joy, *Languages in Conflict* (Montreal 1967), 17–21

Montreal

Located at the confluence of the St Lawrence and Ottawa rivers and adjacent to the Richelieu Valley route southward, Montreal became Canada's metropolis after the necessary dredging had permitted ocean-going ships to reach its port. By the census of 1851, the City of Montreal had a population of 57,715, which was well above the population of either Quebec City (42,052) or Toronto (30,775). It might be noted that, at this census, persons of French origin made up only 45 per cent of Montreal's population.

By 1911, Toronto, with a population of 376,538, had far surpassed Quebec City. However, Montreal, which had just annexed several former suburbs, was still Canada's most populous city, with 470,480 residents. Almost 64 per cent of Montrealers were of French origin, and Médéric Martin succeeded Arsène Lavallée as mayor in 1914, breaking the tradition whereby members of the two main language groups had alternated in this post.

An important factor in Montreal's change of ethnic make-up had been the virtual disappearance of the Irish. It is possible that many of the descendants of the Irish immigrants of the previous century were still present and had merely declared their origin as French or English, depending on the language group to which they had assimilated. However, it seems more likely that most of the Irish had moved on to more promising careers elsewhere.

At the 1851 census, Irish-born residents of Montreal had been twice as numerous as the combined total of Montrealers born in England and Scotland. By 1911, however, there were only 36,943 persons in Montreal who declared themselves to be of Irish origin, fewer than 8 per cent of the city's population. Notable among other non-French Montrealers were some 28,000 Jews, reflecting recent immigration from Eastern Europe, and about 7,000 Italians.

The 1941 census reported a population of 1,139,921 for the metropolitan area of Montreal, at that time defined as being the Island of Montreal plus some off-island suburbs. By then, the immigrants of the early part of the century had settled down and the heavy immigration of the post-1945 years had not yet begun.

Almost 63 per cent of the total population (713,522 persons) were of French origin. Just under 25 per cent were of British Isles origin, but only 60,337 of these claimed to be of Irish origin; the latter were outnumbered by the 63,937 Montrealers who were of Jewish origin. The next-largest group was the 25,351 persons of Italian origin; all other origins combined came to about 55,000 persons.

In terms of mother tongue, a question that, in its present form, had just been introduced into the census questionnaire, French was the language of 63.2 per cent of Montreal's population (720,963 persons), English of 26.6 per cent (303,430 persons), Yiddish of 51,023 persons, and Italian of 20,104 persons. As can be seen, there was still a close correspondence between origin and mother tongue: the number of persons who reported English as their mother tongue was only 21,555 higher than the number of those who had given a British Isles origin.

After 1945, large-scale immigration into Canada resumed, and Montreal, being the country's metropolis as well as a major port of entry, attracted many of the foreign-born newcomers. The inflow from abroad was supplemented by some in-migration from the other provinces and by a significant movement of population from the rural areas of Quebec.

By 1971, the enlarged metropolitan area contained 2,743,235 people, of whom 405,685 had been born outside Canada and an additional 154,210 had been born in Canada outside the Province of Quebec. With their children, born in the province, these in-migrants would have made up about one-quarter of the total population of Montreal.

Many of these newcomers did not speak French, as even those who were of non-official mother tongues tended to communicate in English. Thus, despite the fact that over 66 per cent of Montreal's population reported French as the language they spoke most often at home, three aspects of the growth of the census metropolitan area (CMA) genuinely disturbed both professional and amateur Québécois politicians:

- the Montreal CMA had been growing much more rapidly than had the rest of Quebec and, by 1971, contained almost 46 per cent of the province's total population;
- almost 56 per cent of the residents of Montreal claimed to be able to carry on a conversation in English, and there was more pressure on francophones to learn English than on anglos to learn French; and
- 683,390 persons in Montreal reported English as the language they spoke most often at home, compared to only 595,395 who were of English mother tongue and 438,500 who were of British origins.

As has been noted in the previous chapter, there was an exodus of anglos from the province after 1976, and many of these came from Montreal. At the census taken in 1986, there were only 600,360 persons of English home language (496,260 of English mother tongue) living in a Montreal CMA that was larger than that of 1971. In contrast to the sharp decline in numbers of the English-speaking population, the number of Montrealers of French home language had risen from 1,818,865 in 1971 to 2,012,130 in 1986, and those speaking non-official languages in their homes had risen from 240,980 to 308,867. In other words, anglos made up only 20.8 per cent of Montreal's population in 1986, down from 24.9 per cent in 1971, while the proportion of francophones had risen to 69.7 per cent.

Adding to the pressure on the English language, the 1977 legislation strictly limited those who would be permitted to enrol in the province's English schools. Effectively, these regulations forced all immigrants to send their children to French-language schools, regardless of their mother tongues or preferences.

The departure of anglos from Montreal and the reduced status of the English language in that metropolitan area have considerably alleviated the problems highlighted by the 1971 census. All parts of Montreal have been affected by the departures; even in the west end of Montreal Island, where just over two-thirds of the residents were of English mother tongue in 1971, the proportion had dropped to 54 per cent in 1986, and the trend was definitely downward.[2]

Were it not for the shadow cast by sharply lower birth rates among the French-speaking population, there would seem to be no valid reason for further concern about the continuing primacy of the French language in the Montreal area.[3]

However, there has been at least one negative consequence of the departure of so many Montrealers who prefer to live in English. Toronto's population passed that of Montreal in 1976 and is now almost 20 per cent greater than that of the former metropolis; the latter has fallen from its long-time position as hub of Canada's industry and commerce and is now mainly a regional centre.[4]

2 These figures are for eleven contiguous municipalities located on the west end of Montreal Island.

3 See, however, Michel Paillé, *Nouvelles tendances démolinguistiques dans l'Île de Montréal, 1981–1986* (Quebec City: Conseil de la langue française 1989).

4 For a discussion of the possible consequences, see Gary Caldwell and Daniel Fournier, 'The Quebec Question: A Matter of Population,' *Canadian Journal of Sociology* 12/1–2 (1987), 16–41

The North and East

Although three-quarters of Quebec's anglos live within the Montreal CMA, those elsewhere in the province number just under 200,000 persons.[5] The majority of these are in the Gatineau area or in the Eastern Townships, as previously noted, but approximately 65,000 anglos live in the north and east of the province.[6]

A major concentration is to be found in the Quebec City CMA. Here the minority is now only 3 per cent of the total population, but its members still have access to medical, educational, and other services in their own language. The trend is definitely downwards, since the 1861 census reported approximately 30,000 persons of British Isles origins living in Quebec City and County, compared to only 16,000 anglos in 1986, although the total population of the area had risen from 80,000 in 1861 to 600,000 in 1986.

Approximately 11,000 anglos live in the Gaspé Peninsula, mainly along the north side of the Baie des Chaleurs. The other significant concentration is in Saguenay County, where 7,000 are to be found north of the Gulf of St Lawrence. Two urban communities are worth noting: 5,000 in the lower St Maurice valley and just over 3,000 in Chicoutimi County. The remainder are scattered throughout the rest of the region.

In a study written for the Conseil de la langue française, Gary Caldwell has drawn attention to a qualitative weakness of the anglo communities outside Montreal: 'On ne trouve pas d'éléments capables de créer ou de soutenir un sentiment d'appartenance.'[7] According to Caldwell, there is an almost complete absence of leaders in these communities, if one excepts the school staffs who, he states, are too busy looking after their own interests and cannot safeguard the interests of the rest of the community. The selective out-migration of potential leaders has also weakened the minority groups.

My own experience leads me to add another comment. Even thirty

---

5 'Adjusted language data,' published by Statistics Canada, show that, in 1986, there were, in Quebec province, outside the Montreal CMA: 196,335 persons of English home language, including 161,130 who had given the single response 'English'; and 182,525 persons of English mother tongue, including 146,935 who had given the single response 'English.'
6 'Approximately,' depending on the manner in which multiple responses are allocated to 'English,' 'French,' etc.
7 Gary Caldwell, *Le Québec anglophone hors de la région de Montréal dans les anneés soixante-dix* (Quebec City: Conseil de la langue française 1980), 37

years ago, the French-language universities of Quebec were not turn-ing out the graduates required by the province's industries. It was necessary to bring in trained people from outside Quebec, and one of the accepted costs of recruiting such a predominantly English-speaking group was that of providing schools and other services in the English language. This situation no longer exists and, although special exceptions to the educational provisions of Bill 101 are some-times negotiated by companies considering significant investment in Quebec, there is no longer a heavy inflow of English-speaking families who must be provided with facilities in their own preferred language.

The future of Quebec's minority-language communities is less than promising, even in Montreal. Outside Montreal, the prospects are particularly poor in the north and east of the province, where the communities are small and not in touch with English-speakers in Ontario or the United States and where the French language is un-questionably dominant. Of the 2.4 million total population of this region, 65,000 Anglos represent only 2.7 per cent, which may not be high enough to ensure survival of the English language.

The Northern Peninsula

Reference has been made to the inhabited area of Quebec province. In contrast, the northern portion of the province is very sparsely populated and should be discussed separately.

In 1898, following surveys of the area, the federal parliament and the Quebec legislature agreed that the province's northern limit should follow a line eastward from James Bay along the Eastmain River. This line was generous to Quebec, but the agreement could be described as merely the resolution of a long-standing uncertainty. In any case, almost 62 per cent of the population of this area told the 1986 census that they spoke 'French only' – most of them lived in towns such as Chibougamau and Lebel-sur-Quévillon – and there were only a few thousand Natives (mainly Indians) in Nouveau-Québec, south of the Eastmain.

In 1912, however, the federal government made a gift to Quebec of all the land (formerly, part of the Northwest Territories) between the 1898 line and Hudson Strait.[8] Within this area, despite some in-migration from the south, the language profile of the population is quite different from that of the rest of the province, as shown by the

8 The Quebec Boundaries Extension Act, 1912

following figures on language spoken: 'English only,' 3,900; 'English + French,' 700; 'French only,' 1,300; neither official language, 2,900 (total population in 1986, 8,800 persons).[9] The possibility of this northern area rejoining the Northwest Territories is discussed in chapter 19.

9 These figures calculated from 1986 census data for subdivisions of the census division Territoire-du-Nouveau-Québec

16

Ontario: The Province

The first French post in what is now Ontario was established in 1639, three years before the founding of Montreal. Sainte-Marie, located on Georgian Bay just east of the present city of Midland, was built to serve the Jesuit missions to the Hurons, but survived for only ten years before being abandoned in response to Iroquois pressure from the south.

For the remainder of the French regime, Ontario seems to have been regarded as merely a pathway to the interior of the continent. To reach the Great Lakes, French fur traders, missionaries, and military men followed either the southern route, via Kingston (Fort Frontenac) to Niagara, or the northern route, which went up the Ottawa River and across into Georgian Bay.

The one noteworthy exception to this general indifference appears to have been the colony around Lake St Clair, centred on the French post established at Detroit about 1701. (This, incidentally, calls attention to one of the geographical problems that can arise in a discussion of this sort, since many of the colonists were located in what became the State of Michigan and only part of the settlement was in what is now Ontario.)

By 1791, the United Empire Loyalists were firmly established along the St Lawrence River west of Montreal. They requested (and were given) their own system of government, distinct from that of the French Canadians in Lower Canada. The line drawn at that time remains, with only minor changes, the boundary between Ontario and Quebec.

The Loyalists were followed by other Americans eager to make their fortunes and indifferent as to the flag that waved over them.

For example, the seigneury of Longueil was purchased in 1796 by Nathaniel Treadwell, from Plattsburgh, who founded the village of Treadwell and brought in settlers from New York and the New England states.

The War of 1812 and subsequent adjustments to the border between Ontario and the United States resulted in some slight changes in the settlement pattern. The right bank of the St Clair River, including Detroit, had become an undisputed part of the United States. Farther north, British forces withdrawing from Drummond Island and Michilimackinac brought with them some fur traders, and francophones among the latter became the progenitors of today's French-speaking enclave around Penetanguishene.

At the 1851 census of the Canadas, Upper Canada had a total population of 952,004. Of these, 176,267 had been born in Ireland; 158,510 in England, Scotland, and Wales; 43,732 in the United States; 9,957 in Germany and Holland; and only 1,007 in France and Belgium. Adding the last number to the 26,417 persons of French-origin who had been born in Canada, it would appear that the French-origin population of Ontario then amounted to about 27,400 persons, not quite 3 per cent of the total population.

In 1851, just over one-quarter of Ontario's French population was living in the southwest (Essex and Kent counties), approximately 7,000 were in Bytown and the three counties along the lower Ottawa River, and 569 were in Simcoe County, on Georgian Bay. The cities of the south had only small French populations, and even Stormont County was barely 5 per cent French.

Subsequent decades saw a substantial flow of migrants from Quebec, who came into the lower and upper Ottawa Valley and into eastern Ontario as far as Cornwall. This influx was facilitated by the departure of many of the English-speaking people who had previously farmed the area; they left to seek better lands or more promising careers in the west of Ontario or in the United States.

By 1901, there were 158,671 persons of French origin in Ontario, 7.3 per cent of the total population. Although 21,638 of these were in the southwest of the province (Essex North and South, and Kent counties), the Lake St Clair region was losing its former role as the focal point of French Ontario. This role was being taken over by Ottawa, where Archbishop J.-T. Duhamel, a strong proponent of the French language, was making sure that the newcomers from Quebec had parishes and schools in their own language.

In January 1910, there was a great 'Congrès Canadien-français' in Ottawa, attended by some 1,200 delegates from all parts of Ontario requesting the teaching of French, in addition to English, in all the 'arrondissements où nous sommes en majorité.' Premier James Whitney, a Conservative, and his colleagues did not attend the congress, and the requests were not favourably received, even though the prime minister of Canada, Sir Wilfrid Laurier, had been conspicuously present at the public meeting held as part of the congress.

At the census of 1911, there were 202,442 persons of French origin in Ontario, 8 per cent of the province's total population. Despite this, or perhaps because of it, the Conservative government of Premier Whitney approved Regulation 17, which effectively made teaching in French illegal after the first or second year of school.[1]

Organizations both inside and outside the province protested the imposition of Regulation 17, and money was collected in Quebec to help support the French-language schools of Ontario. However, Whitney was successful in his bid for re-election in 1914, winning 83 seats against only 26 for the Liberals, and it was not until 1927 that Regulation 17 finally became a dead letter.

Despite this setback, the French-origin population of Ontario continued to grow, in relative strength as well as in numbers. By 1941, there were 374,000 persons of French origin in the province, just under 10 per cent of the total population. The proportion peaked at 10.4 per cent in 1951 and 1961, before falling off in 1971 as postwar immigration began to quicken.

However, two new census questions showed that anglicization had become a major factor in reducing the French-speaking minority in Ontario. As can be seen from table 12, by 1971 Ontario residents who reported French as the language they spoke most often in their own homes represented less than half the number of those who were of French origin.

More recently, another factor has been reducing the relative strength of the official-language minority in Ontario. As was shown in table 7, the number of school-aged children of French mother tongue dropped drastically between 1971 and 1986, and their proportion among the 0–14 age group fell from 8.5 per cent in 1951 to only 4.3 per cent in 1986. Reflecting the continuing decline in birth rates, the

---

1 'Instructions No. 17,' its formal title, was dated June 1912, and came into force at the beginning of the 1912–13 school year.

TABLE 12
Province of Ontario, total population and 'French' population, censuses of 1871 to 1986
(adjusted data)

Census	Total population	'French' population	'French'/ Total (%)
1871 EO[a]	1,621[d]	75	4.7
1901 EO	2,183	159	7.3
1931 EO	3,432	300	8.7
1951 EO	4,598	478	10.4
MT[b]	4,598	342	7.4
1971 EO	7,703	737	9.6
MT	7,703	482	6.3
HL[c]	7,703	352	4.6
1986 MT	9,102	484	5.3
HL	9,001[e]	341[f]	3.8

[a]   EO = 'by ethnic origin.'
[b]   MT = 'by mother tongue.'
[c]   HL = 'by home language.'
[d]   All numbers are in thousands.
[e]   The total population shown for Ontario in 1986 did not include an estimated
      11,821 persons living on non-cooperating Indian reserves. The number used
      when calculating the proportion of persons of French home language was
      9,001,160; this figure excludes inmates of institutions as well as the non-cooper-
      ating Indians.
[f]   The 'French' population in 1986 included only 281,615 persons (3.1 per cent of
      the total population) who replied 'French' to the census question on home lan-
      guage; the figure of 340,545 is as published by Statistics Canada after allocation
      of all multiple responses.

proportion among the 0–4 age group (including an allocation of multiple responses) was only 4 per cent.

Of the nine million people in Ontario at the time of the 1986 census,
only 281,615 replied 'French' when asked which language they were
speaking most often in the home. Even the 'adjusted' figure (340,545)
published by Statistics Canada represented only 3.8 per cent of the
province's population, so the relative strength of Ontario's francophone minority has fallen back to a level not seen in over a century.

Unless there is a substantial increase in the birth rates of French-
speaking families and/or significant net migration of francophones
into Ontario from Quebec or elsewhere, the Franco-Ontarian popu-

lation will continue to decline in relative strength and, perhaps, even in absolute numbers.

Despite the downward trend shown by the census figures, the recent Liberal government of David Peterson enacted three major laws intended to encourage use of the French language in Ontario.

By legislation (Bill 75) passed in 1986, the Education Act was amended to provide for minority-language sections of each school-board, responsible for all matters affecting only the minority-language schools of that board. As a result, the courses for French-language students will in future be set by French-language (as defined in the Bill) trustees.

Bill 8, also passed in 1986, provided for French-language services by the government of Ontario and by certain other organizations, including those municipalities that so decide. One of the more important of its provisions is that any person may use the French language in communications with the head or central office of any government agency and with any office serving an area designated in the schedule to the bill. (The bill specified no criteria for listing in the schedule, and the Office of Francophone Affairs was given a free hand to designate areas in which French-language services must be offered. Included was every municipality that, at the 1981 census, was reported by Statistics Canada, after allocation of all multiple responses, to have had at least 5,000 persons, or 10 per cent of its population, of French mother tongue. Also listed were a few municipalities [for example, the City of Pembroke] that did not meet even these minima. New areas may be added to the schedule at any time, by the lieutenant governor in council, but deletions can be effected only by a vote of the legislature.)

The third major piece of legislation, passed in mid-1988, established a French-language school-board in Ottawa-Carleton to take over all the French-language schools of the four existing boards. Details of this bill will be found in chapter 10.

It should be noted, however, that the preceding Conservative government, in 1984,[2] decided not to appeal the Ontario Court of Appeal's interpretation of section 23 of the Canadian Charter of Rights and Freedoms; this gave the French-speaking minorities the right to control their own schools and opened the way for subsequent legislation.

2 *Reference Re Education Act of Ontario* (1984), 10 DLR (4th) 491

Only time will tell whether these various laws can reverse the trends that have been so evident during the past forty years (see table 12). Meanwhile, considerable publicity has been given to the 1986 census report that 1,113,100 persons in Ontario claimed that they could carry on a conversation in French, well up from the 808,915 of 1971.

Seldom mentioned is the fact that the total population of Ontario had also grown considerably between 1971 and 1986, so the increase in the number of 'parlants-français' is not nearly as impressive as it might seem at first glance. The 1986 figure is only 12.4 per cent of the total population, just under one person in eight, while the proportion in 1971 had been 10.5 per cent. With seven out of eight of its residents unable to converse in French, Ontario still has a long way to go before it can call itself reasonably bilingual, in any sense except the legal one.

The Regions
Although the preceding pages have discussed the province as a whole, any study of the French language in Ontario must take into account the fact that the situation in the north and east of the province is quite different from that in the south and centre. The various regions of Ontario will be discussed in the next chapter.

17

Ontario: The Regions

Even the most superficial examination of the language characteristics of Ontario requires that the province be divided into two quite distinct regions.[1] The north and east of the province represents the westward extension of Quebec; many French-speaking families moved into the Ottawa Valley and northern Ontario during the late 1800s and early 1900s.[2] This region is made up of the regional municipalities of Ottawa-Carleton and Sudbury and the counties (or equivalents) of Algoma, Cochrane, Glengarry, Nipissing, Prescott, Renfrew, Russell, Stormont, Sudbury, and Timiskaming.

At the most recent census, that of 1986, not quite 15 per cent of Ontario's population was living in the north and east of the province. However, this region was home to 81 per cent of all Ontarians who had given the single response 'French' to the 'home language' census question.

In the north and east, persons of French home language represented approximately 20 per cent of the total population, after allocating all multiple responses. In the rest of Ontario, fewer than 1 per cent of the population reported French as the language they spoke most often in their own homes. Quite obviously, a language spoken by one-fifth of the voters and consumers living in a region has a more important status than one spoken by not even one person in a hundred.

This difference in status is amplified by the fact that the only major urban centre in the border region – Ottawa – depends heavily on an

---

1 Cf. Richard J. Joy, *Canada's Official-Language Minorities* (Montreal: C.D. Howe Research Institute 1978), 16–20.
2 Cf. Richard J. Joy, *Languages in Conflict* (Montreal 1967), 118–22.

TABLE 13
Population of French home language in the north and east of Ontario and elsewhere
in the province, censuses of 1971, 1981, and 1986

Region	1971	1981[a]	1986[a]
North & East	280,730	266,155	265,000 ± [b]
Elsewhere	71,735	66,780	76,000 ± [b]

[a] Data exclude 'inmates of institutions.'
[b] Multiple responses in 1986 have been allocated by the author and, as noted, are
subject to some error.

employer, the federal government, that has a stated policy of encouraging the use of the French language. Although certain jobs in
the south require a knowledge of French, there is not the same pressure on employees to learn this particular language (French placed
only seventh among the mother tongues reported by residents of
Toronto in 1986).

Anglicization has been far heavier in the south and west than it
has been in the north and east. *Canada's Official-Language Minorities*
analysed data from the 1971 census to show that there was a wide
range in the degree of anglicization apparent in the ten subregions
into which Ontario could be divided.[3] In the first three of these subregions, those located in the north and east of the province, there were
398,215 persons of French ethnic origin and 280,730 of French home
language, a difference of only 30 per cent. However, in the remaining
seven subregions, the figures were 339,145 and 71,735, respectively,
with a difference of 79 per cent.

Partly as a result of this anglicization and partly of interprovincial
migration patterns that saw many families move from Quebec into
the Ottawa Valley and northern Ontario, the north and east has re-
placed the southwest as the centre of the French language in Ontario.
Table 13 presents data from the three censuses at which respondents
were asked to report the language they spoke most often in their own
homes. (This table updates the information presented in Table 63 of
Languages in Conflict, which presented the data from 1871 to 1961.)

To illustrate the differences between the two regions, their principal
cities, Ottawa and Toronto, are discussed below. Researchers will, of

3 Joy, *Canada's Official-Language Minorities*, Table 8

course, wish to make their own studies of the rural areas and of the smaller cities.

Ottawa

One-quarter of Ontario's francophones live within the census metropolitan area of Ottawa, the major urban centre of the north and east. Here, use of the French language at work is encouraged by the city's largest employer, the federal government, and services in both official languages are offered by both the provincial and the municipal governments. Also, as has been described in a previous chapter, all French-language schools are administered by their own board.

Languages in Conflict (1967) pointed out that Ottawa had become the focal point of French-language activities in Ontario. Within the city could be found the three pillars of Franco-Ontarian prestige: the archdiocese, the university, and the daily newspaper. These institutions still exist, but all three have been seriously weakened during the past two decades.

The archdiocese has suffered from the general decline in religious fervour but has been particularly affected by the constantly decreasing proportion of French-speakers among Ottawa's Catholics. In 1981 (at the most recent census to ask a question on religion), there were 258,505 Catholics in Ottawa-Carleton, but only 84,280 persons who reported French as the language they were speaking most often at home. The Archdiocese of Ottawa had been under the control of francophones for most of its existence but, when Marcel Gervais was appointed to succeed Joseph-Aurèle Plourde, interviews in the *Ottawa Citizen* stressed the incoming archbishop's fluency in the English language.

The University of Ottawa has historically been regarded as the region's 'French' university (Carleton has always been predominantly 'English') and, as recently as 1972, francophones made up 59 per cent of the student body. However, the French-speaking proportion of student registration has now dropped to below 40 per cent, and there have been some calls for formation of a new university that will be 'French' and not, as at present, 'bilingual.'[4]

The daily *Le Droit* was founded in 1913 and was owned by the Oblate order for its first seventy years. It was initiated to fight for

4 Gisèle Goudreault, 'A French-Language University in Ontario,' *Language and Society* 29 (Winter 1989), 20–1

TABLE 14
'French' and total populations of Ottawa-Carleton,[a] censuses of 1931 to 1986

Census year	Total population	'French' population	'French'/ Total (%)
1931 EO[b]	170,040	48,100	28.3
1951 EO	242,247	70,997	29.3
MT[c]	''	63,118	26.1
1971 EO	471,930	117,465	24.9
MT	''	97,975	20.8
HL[d]	''	82,700	17.5
1986 MT	606,639	113,000 ±[f]	18.6
HL[e]	600,545	90,000 ±[f]	14.9

[a] Data for 1931 and 1951 are for Carleton County; data for 1971 and 1986 are for Ottawa-Carleton.
[b] EO = 'by ethnic origin.'
[c] MT = 'by mother tongue.'
[d] HL = 'by home language.'
[e] 1986 HL data exclude inmates of institutions.
[f] Multiple responses in 1986 have been allocated by the author and are subject to some (probably slight) error.

what were regarded as the rights of Franco-Ontarians, but two-thirds of its readers now live in Quebec and are not personally affected by events that are of importance to the French-speaking minority of Ontario.

The local geography has been both a help and a hindrance to the French-speaking minority. Since they tend to live in the northeast of the metropolitan area, members of their own language group are certain to be elected to both Parliament and the provincial legislature. However, when the population of Ottawa increased and expanded into the suburbs, families from French-speaking areas tended to move right out of the province into new subdivisions across the Ottawa River, while the non-French remained with Ontario.

The results of the various movements of population and of the recent sharp decline in French birth rates can be seen from table 14.

Despite the continuing deterioration of their relative position, the francophones of Ottawa-Carleton (and, of course, those of the other border counties of northern and eastern Ontario) are still far better off than their colinguists who are now living in the south and west of the provinces. To illustrate the situation in this latter region, a description of Toronto will be given, followed by brief comments on the Windsor area and the three census divisions located west of the Great Lakes.

Toronto

Ontario's recent growth has been most pronounced in the south of the province, particularly within the metropolitan area of Toronto. The 1986 census reported a population of 3,427,168 for the Toronto census metropolitan area (CMA); this figure was almost double that for the population counted in 1961 and places Toronto clearly ahead of Montreal as Canada's most populous metropolitan area.

Toronto's population includes a high proportion of immigrants, and half a million residents of the metropolitan area told the 1986 census that they spoke a non-official language in their own homes. The most popular of these languages was Italian, spoken by 119,530 people, followed by Chinese (84,575), Portuguese (54,405), Greek (29,530), Spanish (19,720), and Polish (18,665). The single response 'French' was given by 16,890 persons, 0.5 per cent of the total population.[5]

The position of Toronto's French-speaking minority is not helped by the fact that this group is far from homogeneous. An enquiry made by Ronald Sabourin, professor of sociology at Glendon College, found that fewer than 20 per cent of Toronto's francophones had been born in Ontario. Close to 30 per cent had been born outside Canada, and the great majority of the remainder were from Quebec, often people who had been posted to business or government offices in Toronto for two- to five-year tours of duty.[6] It is an interesting commentary on the diversity of this French-speaking group, having only language as a common factor, that the Association multiculturelle francophone de l'Ontario (AMFO) has the majority of its members in Toronto, rather than in the northeast of the province.[7]

It must be underlined that some 300,000 residents of Toronto claim

---

5 All these numbers are single responses, as shown by Statistics Canada, in *Language: Part 2*, Catalogue no. 93-103 (Ottawa 1989).
6 François Brousseau, 'Les Franco-Torontois en chiffres,' *Le Droit*, 4 January 1988, 18
7 The AMFO's president is Pierre-Eddy Toussaint, and members are from a score of countries, including France, Belgium, Switzerland, Morocco, Haiti, and Egypt: *Coup d'oeil*, February 1988, 2.

to be able to carry on a conversation in French.[8] This represents only 8.8 per cent of the population of the metropolitan area, but the absolute number is quite impressive and is often mentioned.

Toronto is Canada's most populous metropolitan area, the seat of the provincial government, and the centre of Canadian industry and commerce. For these reasons, Toronto has been designated, at both the federal and the provincial level, as a city in which government offices must be capable of offering their services in French as well as in English. Since 1988, it has also been the centre of Ontario activities of the office of the (federal) commissioner of official languages.

The Southwest

There has been a long history of French settlement in the Lake St Clair area, the site of today's Detroit and Windsor. In 1791, when Canada was split, there was serious consideration given to having this area become, in effect, an enclave subject to the laws of Lower Canada. As noted in chapter 16, the southwest remained the focal point of the French language in Ontario until well on into the nineteenth century.

However, the situation here has changed drastically in recent decades as anglicization exerted pressure from the Detroit side of the boundary as well as from the Ontario side. Under Bill 8, the City of Windsor, several townships along Lake St Clair, and three municipalities in Kent County are included in the schedule that designates areas that must receive French-languages services. However, it would no longer be possible to propose a bilingual district that would include the City of Windsor and also meet the (1969) federal requirement that at least 10 per cent of the population of the district be of French mother tongue.

The 1986 census found only 7,745 persons in Essex, Kent, and Lambton counties who gave the single response 'French' to the 'home language' question. Even after adding an allowance for those who had given a multiple response that included French, it is unlikely that there are now more than 10,000 francophones in the entire area, less than 2 per cent of the total population. Comparing this number with the 16,185 persons of French home language at the 1971 census, it appears safe to say that the recent trend has been downward.

8 This figure is from the 1986 census. The same source reports that 1,667,030 residents of Montreal claim to be able to converse in English.

West of the Great Lakes
The three census divisions of Ontario that are located west of the Great Lakes had a total population in 1986 of 231,378 (not counting the residents of several Indian reserves who refused to cooperate with the census enumerators). The metropolis of this area is the CMA of Thunder Bay, which had a 1986 population of 122,217.

The Second Bilingual Districts Advisory Board recommended that a narrow strip along the northwest shore of Lake Superior be designated bilingual, so that the city of Thunder Bay could be included in the bilingual district of Laurentian.[9] This recommendation was made, although the report of the board notes that only 2.2 per cent of the population of Thunder Bay was of French mother tongue. The recommendation was, of course, not adopted.

In the schedule to Bill 8, seven small municipalities in the Thunder Bay census division and one in Kenora are listed, and bilingual provincial services must be made available to their 18,609 residents, of which about 20 per cent are of French mother tongue. However, the City of Thunder Bay does not appear on the schedule.

Since the total population of these three census divisions is only 2.5 per cent of the population of Ontario, the area can, for most purposes, be included in data for the centre and south of the province, despite the geographical contortions that this requires.

9 Second Bilingual Districts Advisory Board, *Report* (Ottawa 1975), 123–5

18

The West

The pattern of settlement in Canada was, generally, from east to west, with the oldest settlements located on the Atlantic Coast and in the St Lawrence Valley. While cities were being established in locations such as Montreal, Toronto, and Quebec, the area west of the Great Lakes was inhabited only by Indians and by a few traders who came in via either Montreal or Hudson Bay. Lord Selkirk's attempt to settle the Red River area in 1811 was unsuccessful, and large-scale home-steading did not begin until the final decades of the nineteenth century.

Although British Columbia was also unsettled until well on into the nineteenth century, a distinction must be made between the Prairies and the area west of the Rocky Mountains. The latter area attracted immigrants who entered Canada via the Pacific route; the characteristics of such immigrants often differed from those of the settlers on the prairies.

All three of the Prairie provinces benefited from completion of the transcontinental railway in the late 1880s, which permitted immigrants to be carried speedily and in relative comfort from eastern ports to their western destinations. Between 1891 and 1901, the population of Manitoba rose from 152,506 to 255,211. At the census taken in 1911, the three Prairie provinces had a total population of over 1.3 million.

At the census of 1911, only 74,020 residents of the Prairie provinces were of French origin, less than 6 per cent of the total population, while 710,123 (54 per cent) were of British origins. This set the dominant language and culture, into which newcomers tended to assimilate. As shown by table 15, barely half the residents of the three

TABLE 15
Places of birth of inhabitants of Manitoba, Saskatchewan, and Alberta, census of 1911

Place of birth	Manitoba	Saskatchewan	Alberta
Province of residence	170,819	101,854	73,813
Other west[a]	2,764	23,026	8,714
Ontario	73,077	96,206	57,530
Quebec	10,755	12,969	10,112
Atlantic[b]	7,616	14,863	12,068
Total Canada	265,031	248,918	162,237
United States	16,326	69,628	81,357
British Isles	90,622	76,854	65,839
Other Europe	78,051	91,104	58,771
Elsewhere	5,584	5,928	6,459
Total population	455,614	492,432	374,663

Source: 1911 Census, vol. 2, Table XVII

[a]   Four western provinces, including British Columbia
[b]   Three Maritime provinces, plus Newfoundland

provinces had been born in Canada, and only 26 per cent had been born in their province of residence.

It is worth noting that immigrants from continental Europe were almost as numerous as those born in the British Isles. Austria and Russia were the nominal countries of birth of many of these newcomers, but, at that time, the two empires covered much of Eastern Europe, including Poland. The United States contributed heavily to the population of Saskatchewan and Alberta, much less so to that of Manitoba.

Among the provinces, Ontario stood out. Quebec did very poorly, and it must be kept in mind that many of the migrants from that province would have been anglos from Montreal or the Townships, or elsewhere; as has been mentioned earlier, fewer than 6 per cent of the inhabitants of the three Prairie provinces were of French origin, and these included 10,128 immigrants from France and Belgium, as well as persons born in the west, so there could have been very few migrants of French origin from eastern Canada.

This failure of French-speakers to move west has been the subject of much discussion. During the critical period, the latter part of the nineteenth century, there was excess population in Quebec. However, most of those who left that province chose to go south, to work in the mill towns of the United States, rather than heading west to the much more distant prairies. The census data speak for themselves: between 1871 and 1911, when the four western provinces were acquiring their distinctive characters, there were very few French colonists.

With persons of British origins forming the majority of the population, it was not surprising that immigrants from Eastern Europe felt a need to learn the English language. This feeling was reinforced by a decision made within the Catholic church: on 10 September 1910, Cardinal Bourne, Archbishop of Westminster, used the occasion of a speech in Notre Dame Church, in Montreal, to announce that English would thenceforth be the language of the church in western Canada.[1]

Although this comment is out of chronological sequence, it should be noted that the 1981 census (the most recent to include a question on religion) found 1,242,755 Catholics in the three Prairie provinces but only 70,675 persons who reported French as the language they spoke most often at home. This means that fewer than 6 per cent of the Catholics in the Prairie provinces are francophones. In British Columbia, the proportion is below 3 per cent.

The trend that had become so obvious by 1910 has continued, with a minimal, and decreasing, French presence west of Ontario. The proportion of the population of the Prairie provinces who were of French mother tongue had slipped to 5 per cent in the 1930s and was down to barely 3 per cent in 1986. By that most recent census, only 63,655 persons in the three provinces reported French as the language they were speaking most often in their own homes; this was less than half the 131,740 of French mother tongue and shows the strength of anglicization in the region. Table 16 shows the decline of French over the years 1931 to 1986.

Manitoba

Three years after Confederation, Canada purchased the Northwest Territories from the Hudson's Bay Company. In that same year, the Province of Manitoba was created, in the southeast corner of the newly acquired land.

The first census of Manitoba was taken in November 1870. The results of this census must be used only with caution, since the census

1 See, in particular, *Le Devoir*, 14 September 1910, 1.

TABLE 16

'French' population vs total population, three prairie provinces, censuses of 1931 to 1986 (adjusted data)

Census year	Total population	'French' population	'French' Total (%)
1931 MT[a]	2,353,529	112,918	4.8
1951 MT	2,547,770	125,210	4.9
1971 MT	3,542,360	116,140	3.3
HL[b]	3,542,360	78,230	2.2
1986 MT	4,438,465	131,740	3.0
HL	4,386,255	63,655[c]	1.5

[a] MT = 'by mother tongue.'
[b] HL = 'by home language.'
[c] In 1986, there were 48,150 single responses 'French' to the 'home language' question; the 63,655 shown includes Statistics Canada's allocation of a portion of the multiple resposes that included 'French.'

covered only twenty-four parishes located along the Red and Assiniboine rivers and did not include the probably more numerous population that would have been found elsewhere, within the present limits of the province, and the enumerators reported approximately 1,600 'Whites' (origins not given), 570 'Christian Indians,' 5,700 'French Half-breeds,' and 4,100 'English Half-breeds.' No question was asked regarding mother tongue or language spoken in the home, and the most that can be inferred from this census is that English and French were about equally spoken. There was no indication of the number of persons who may have favoured Cree or some other Amerindian language.[2]

Since it was expected that the province would attract French-speaking settlers from Quebec, section 23 of the Manitoba Act (1870) was a virtual copy of section 133 of the British North America Act, 1867. This section provided that both the English and the French language should be used in the legislature and in the courts of Manitoba, and that the acts of the legislature should be printed and published in both languages.

However, it soon became apparent that Manitoba would not de-

2 Adams G. Archibald, despatch sent from Government House, Fort Garry, 26 December 1870, in *Sessional Papers No. 20* (Ottawa 1871), 95

velop as a bilingual province. The census of 1885–6 confirmed that settlers had come chiefly from English-speaking areas; these included 34,121 persons from Ontario, 19,925 from the British Isles, and 2,322 from the United States.[3] Meanwhile, the French-speaking element of Manitoba's population was actually declining, as many Métis moved farther west.

In 1885–6, Manitoba's population of 108,640 included only 6,821 'French' and 4,368 'French half-breeds'; the two together made up barely more than 10 per cent of the total population. The 1891 census did not report origins, but stated that only 7.3 per cent of Manitoba's population was French-speaking.[4]

This last figure shows how weak the French language had become by 1890, when the provincial government decreed that, 'so far as the Legislature had jurisdiction to enact,' the English language alone would be used in the records and journals of the Legislative Assembly and in the pleadings and process of the courts. In other words, the guarantees given to the French language by section 23 of the (federal) Manitoba Act were revoked by this provincial law. At about the same time, several related actions were taken by the provincial government.[5]

It was not until 13 December 1979 that the Supreme Court of Canada handed down a judgment declaring invalid the provincial law of 1890. Shortly afterwards, a resident of Manitoba, Roger Bilodeau, appealed a traffic ticket on the grounds that the underlying legislation had been passed in English only and was therefore not valid.[6]

On 16 May 1983, just a few days before the Supreme Court was scheduled to hear the *Bilodeau* case, Prime Minister Trudeau announced that there had been discussions between the federal government, the provincial government, and the Société franco-manitobaine and that the province would soon declare itself bilingual. The statement may or may not have been correct; what is known is that the announcement was made in French only, it did not appear in the text of the prime minister's speech, and it was not picked up

3 Janice Staples, 'Consociationalism at the Provincial Level: The Erosion of Dualism in Manitoba, 1870–1890,' in Kenneth D. McRae, ed., *Consociational Democracy* (Toronto: McClelland and Stewart 1974), 291
4 1891 Census of Canada, *Bulletin No. 11*, 10
5 Staples, 'Consociationalism,' 292–9
6 *A.G. Man.* v. *Forest* [1979] 2 SCR 1032; *Bilodeau* v. *A.G. Man.* [1981] 5 WWR 393

by the English-language media until they had read about it in the French-language press.[7]

In Manitoba, the reaction was immediate and hostile. After a series of referendums at the local level had shown overwhelming popular opposition to the measure, the bill, which had been presented by the government of Howard Pawley, was allowed to die on the order paper of the Legislature.

At present, the laws of Manitoba are being translated into French, in accordance with the decision of the Supreme Court.[8] However, the 1986 census (with all multiple responses allocated to single languages) reported that the province had only 29,765 persons of French home language in a total population of 1,049,325; the proportion was down to 2.8 per cent.

The future is hardly promising for the French-speaking minority in Manitoba.[9] In 1951, there were 6,391 children (aged 0 to 4) of French mother tongue in the province, 7.1 per cent of the total population of that age group. At the 1986 census, the number of such children was down to 2,527, and the proportion to 3.2 per cent. If birth rates remain low and if anglicization continues to erode the French-speaking communities, the decline of Manitoba's official-language minority can only accelerate, unless there should be a substantial in-migration of francophones from Quebec or elsewhere. The probability of this occurring does not seem high.

Saskatchewan and Alberta

Although a separate province of Manitoba had been set up as soon as the area was acquired by Canada, the provinces of Saskatchewan and Alberta were not carved out of the Northwest Territories until 1905. As has been noted earlier in this chapter, the Prairies received many settlers during the early years of this century but the majority were English-speaking, and those from continental Europe tended to learn English as quickly as possible after their arrival in North America.

By 1911, Saskatchewan and Alberta had populations of 492,432 and 374,663, respectively, and these numbers almost doubled during the next twenty years, reaching 921,785 and 731,605 by the census of 1931.

7 See, for example, *Gazette* (Montreal), 19 May 1983, 1.
8 *Reference Re Manitoba Language Rights* [1985] 2 SCR 347
9 Charles Castonguay, 'L'effitement est inévitable,' *Le Droit*, 5 October 1983, 3

The depression had a particularly harsh effect on the western provinces. Alberta's growth slowed drastically, the population rising to only 796,169 in 1941, while Saskatchewan's population actually declined, to 895,992. At that census, 43,728 persons in Saskatchewan (4.9 per cent of the total population) and 31,451 in Alberta (4.0 per cent) reported French as their mother tongue, but languages such as German and Ukrainian were more common on the western prairies than was French.

Although there were lawyers who claimed that certain provisions of the North-West Territories Act provided for obligatory use of the French language in Saskatchewan and Alberta, the legislatures of these two provinces functioned only in English, and laws were passed in that language only.

Successive censuses showed the decline of the French-speaking minorities in the two provinces. At the 1971 census, only 15,930 persons in Saskatchewan and 22,700 in Alberta reported French as the language they were speaking most often in their own homes – 1.7 per cent and 1.4 per cent, respectively, of the total populations of the two provinces.

The adjusted data of the 1986 census showed that only 8,980 persons in Saskatchewan (0.9 per cent of the total population of approximately one million) and 24,910 persons in Alberta (1.1 per cent of 2.34 million) had reported French as the language they were speaking most often in their own homes. Even by the 'mother tongue' data, there had been a sharp drop since 1941, with the proportions only 2.3 per cent and 2.4 per cent, respectively.

This was the background to a Supreme Court ruling, handed down on 25 February 1988,[10] which stated that the nineteenth century legislation was still valid, requiring translation of all laws into French, but that the provincial legislatures were free to repeal or amend this part of the North-West Territories Act.

In April 1988, the Saskatchewan government tabled Bill 2, which provided for introduction of some services in French; however, its main effect was to repeal the need to translate eighty-three years of legislation. Alberta followed shortly afterwards, with a bill that achieved the same effect without making any promises of future French-language services.

These two bills attracted unfavourable media attention for a few

10 *Mercure* v. *A.G. Sask.* [1988] 1 SCR 234

days and then faded from the news. One reason that has been suggested for this lack of opposition is that it was suddenly realized that any attack on the freedom of the western provinces to legislate could be turned into an attack on the power of the Quebec Assemblée nationale to pass legislation such as Bill 101.

British Columbia

Once gold had been discovered in the interior of what is now British Columbia, the authorities in London became seriously concerned that the United States would try to take over the area. After several other forms of government had been tried, a single colony was formed in 1866, uniting the mainland and Vancouver Island. In 1871, this colony became Canada's sixth province. At that time, its population was estimated to have been only 36,247 persons, of whom the great majority would have been Indians.

British Columbia initially grew somewhat more slowly than the three prairie provinces, but its population jumped from 178,657 in 1901 to 392,480 in 1911. Of that latter number, only 8,907 were of French origin, barely more than 2 per cent of the total population, and the influence of the French language was even less here than on the eastern side of the Rockies.

By 1971, when the population of British Columbia had reached 2,184,620, the new question on language spoken at home could find only 11,505 persons who replied 'French'; this was only 0.5 per cent of the total population.

In 1975, the Second Bilingual Districts Advisory Board had this to say about British Columbia: 'So far as the language question is concerned, British Columbia is not a province like the others. The "French fact" in British Columbia has neither the long historical roots which sustain it in other regions of the country nor the significance, visibility and population size clearly apparent in Ontario and New Brunswick as well as in Quebec.'[11]

The second board was, obviously, more realistic than had been its predecessor. The first board, unable to find any area of British Columbia that met even the minimum criteria of the Official Languages Act, nevertheless made the following recommendation: 'Our personal observations, even if they are not supported by statistical data, convinced us that there is an increase in the francophone population in

11 Second Bilingual Districts Advisory Board, *Report* (Ottawa 1975), 163

the cities of Dawson Creek, Prince George, Terrace and Port Alberni. We therefore refer these areas to the next Board which will have at its disposal the census figures of 1971.'[12]

The second board, as is obvious from the text cited earlier, did not find any solace in the data of the 1971 census. In 1981, it might be added, the four cities named by the first board had a total population of 143,976, of which only 3,635 were of French mother tongue; this represents barely one-quarter of the minimum required by law for the cities to be declared bilingual districts.

In 1986, 177,515 inhabitants of British Columbia claimed to be able to carry on a conversation in French. Although this figure is slightly higher than the 155,615 reported by the 1981 census, it is still only 6 per cent of the province's population.

At that same census of 1986, only 10,525 persons in British Columbia gave the single response 'French' when asked what language they spoke most often in their own home; with multiple responses allocated, Statistics Canada has concluded that 17,575 persons (0.6 per cent of the province's population) were of French home language in 1986.

12 First Bilingual Districts Advisory Board, *Report* (Ottawa 1971), 89

19

The Yukon and
the Northwest Territories

Since just over 40 per cent of Canada's land lies north of 60° North latitude, the Yukon and the Northwest Territories, which make up most of this area, cannot be neglected in this book, although their 1986 population totalled only 76,000. However, the high proportion of aboriginal population in the north requires that this chapter follow a rather different pattern from that used in previous chapters describing the provinces of the south.

In the provinces, attention has been focused heavily on the conflict that often exists between the two official languages of Canada. In the territories, however, the principal cultural conflict is one of aboriginal peoples, many speaking their own languages, vs. non-aboriginals, most of whom speak English (according to the *Adjusted Language Data* of the 1986 census, French is the language spoken most often at home by only 275 people in the Yukon and by 755 people in the Northwest Territories).[1]

The territories are far from homogeneous, and there is a distinct gradation visible from southwest to northeast. In the Yukon Territory, the Native influence is weak (their present MP was born and spent much of her life in the south of Canada). The central area is shared by non-Natives and Natives, the latter chiefly Indians and Métis, while the north and east are dominated by Inuit. Table 17 shows the ethnic origins reported by the inhabitants of the territories in 1986.

When discussing Native rights, the Yukon can be virtually disregarded. Raised to the status of a separate territory in 1898, the Yukon

---

1 Statistics Canada, *Adjusted Language Data* (Ottawa, April 1988), with all multiple responses allocated

TABLE 17
Ethnic origins reported by the Native population of the territories, 1986 census[a]

	Yukon	NWT
Total population	23,355	52,020
Native population		
SO[b]	3,280	27,175
MO[c]	1,715	3,355
Inuit, SO only	35	17,385
Indian, SO only	3,165	7,585
Métis, SO only	80	2,200

Source: Statistics Canada, *Profile of Ethnic Groups*, Catalogue no. 93-154 (Ottawa 1989), tables 1 and 2

[a] It should be noted that the 1986 census asked: 'Question 7: Do you consider yourself an aboriginal person or a native Indian of North America, that is, Inuit, North American Indian or Métis?' If this question had been answered in an acceptable manner, there would have been no need to cite the ethnic origin data, as given in this table. However, the results of Q. 7 were sufficiently disappointing that Statistics Canada chose not to publish them (see Statistics Canada, *Census Handbook*, Catalogue no. 99-104E [Ottawa 1988], 89). The question was not asked in 1991.

[b] SO = 'single origin.'

[c] MO = 'multiple origin.': perhaps half of the latter should be counted as members of the ethnic group.

has been peopled chiefly by non-Natives from the south, many of whom came up to look for gold and, later, for other minerals.

In 1986, the Yukon had a population of 23,355. Of these, only some 4,200 were Native people, by the 'ethnic origin' criterion (nearly all North American Indians, with only a handful of Métis and Inuit). Very few of those who considered themselves to be of aboriginal origins had retained their ancient languages, and *Adjusted Language Data* showed that 97 per cent of the population spoke English in their own homes, 1.2 per cent spoke French, and 1.8 per cent spoke non-official languages, including the aboriginal tongues.

In contrast, just over one-third of the population of the Northwest Territories claimed to be of Inuit origin, another 16 per cent were of Indian origin, and just under 6 per cent reported Métis origin. In other words, the Native peoples formed a clear majority in the Northwest Territories.

However, percentage figures can be misleading. The reality is that, although the Northwest Territories occupy just over 35 per cent of

Canada's area, they are home to only 0.2 per cent of the country's population. The total population in 1986 was only 52,245 persons, and this small number could be submerged by a wave of new immigrants attracted by mining or some other activity.

Looking at the 1986 census data, it would appear that the Inuit appear relatively safe in their control of the north and east of the Northwest Territories, and that an Inuit will continue to be elected to Parliament by Nunatsiaq riding.

In the south and west of the Northwest Territories, however, there are settlements of non-Natives in the Yellowknife–Hay River–Fort Smith area, north of the Saskatchewan border, and, to a lesser extent, in the oil camps around Inuvik. Although the present MP from the Western Arctic happens to be a Dene Indian, her successor could be a non-Native.

These factors, particularly the small number of persons in the Northwest Territories, carry serious implications for not only the ethnic origin of elected members but for the results of any referendums taken up there. If it is wished to obtain the views of only the Native population, this must first be defined and then measures must be taken to restrict the voting rights of non-Natives.

Distribution of the Native Peoples

Another factor worth noting is that about 56 per cent of Canada's Inuit (as measured by ethnic origin) live in the Northwest Territories, and an additional 31 per cent live in the Ungava Peninsula (mainly in Quebec but some in Labrador). In sharp contrast, only 2 per cent of Canada's Indians and about 3 per cent of the Métis live in the Northwest Territories, the great majority being found in the south.

The Future of the Northwest Territories

By an order-in-council passed in 1918, the Northwest Territories was divided into three districts. However, the general thinking in recent years, supported by the results of a plebiscite held in 1985, appears to favour a division into two parts: Nunavut, predominantly Inuit, would be north and east of the tree line; and Denendeh, heavily Dene and Métis, would be south and west of the tree line. The exact border between Nunavut and Denendeh has not yet been decided, particularly in the oil-rich Mackenzie Delta; in the near future, another plebescite may be held to set a precise line.

The Ungava Peninsula

In 1912, as has been recounted in a previous chapter, the federal government gave the Territory of Ungava to Quebec; only the islands in James Bay and Hudson Bay were retained by the Northwest Territories.

It is possible that, should Quebec separate from Canada, article 811 of the Civil Code could be invoked to bring about a revocation of the gift. It is also a possibility, if the Civil Code is not invoked, that the people of the peninsula should be allowed to vote on whether they wish to separate from Quebec. However, the total population of this area was only about 9,000 persons in 1986, so a pro-Quebec vote could be favoured by any one of several alternative methods (for example, simply by defining the voting unit as the whole of Nouveau-Québec, wherein persons of French origin made up a majority of the population in 1986).

Incidentally, a clear majority of the population of Labrador, which occupies the eastern part of the peninsula, was of British origins in 1986; that census reported only about 3,000 aboriginals in the census division.

20

Conclusions and Recommendation

The conclusions to *Languages in Conflict*, written in the mid-1960s, warned of the increasing polarization of Canada's two official languages, of the gradual decline of the linguistic minorities, and of the stresses that these trends would place on Canadian unity. This message was repeated, with increased urgency, in the conclusions to *Canada's Official-Language Minorities*.

Since publication of that latter study in 1978, the data of the 1981 and 1986 censuses have confirmed that, whether the criterion be home language or the older mother tongue, the anglo minority of Quebec has fallen in actual numbers, not merely as a percentage of the province's total population. Many English-speakers have moved out of Quebec, relatively few have moved in, and those now to be found in the province do not hold the prestige and influence once characteristic of their language group; the decline has been qualitative as well as quantitative.

This decline cannot be disregarded; although more attention tends to be paid to the French-speaking minorities outside Quebec, it should not be overlooked that Quebec's anglos also have an important role in holding Canada together. The continuing decline of the English language has increased the distinctness of Quebec, the only province with an electorate that is predominantly French-speaking.

Meanwhile, although the number of francophones in Canada has continued to increase, their relative strength, as a proportion of Canada's total population, has been declining. In the 1920s, Abbé Lionel Groulx expressed concern because the proportion of Canadians who were of French origin had dropped from about 31 per cent after Confederation to 27.9 per cent at the census of 1921; today, fewer than

24 per cent of Canada's population are speaking the French language in their homes and the trend has been downwards.

Incidentally, Quebec's relative strength within Canada has been going down, in recent decades, and is now below 25.5 per cent, compared with the 28.9 per cent reported in 1949 (after Newfoundland had joined Confederation).

All these developments can be documented by census data, using the existing questionnaires. To this extent, the census is doing its job satisfactorily. The danger is that members of Parliament and other legislators are not sufficiently alert to the weaknesses of the present census questions, particularly when they are used to measure the linguistic minorities in relatively small areas.

Despite the best efforts of Statistics Canada, the data from the language questions of the 1986 census do not yield a straightforward answer to the administrator's question: to what extent does the population of each municipality wish to be offered service in the minority language? Even when information is collected from the entire population (rather than from only a sample), there are problems related to response errors and other defects, and these problems were compounded in 1986 when multiple responses were actually invited to the 'home language' and 'mother tongue' questions of the census.

What is required is the addition of a completely new question that will ask every Canadian his or her preferred official language. However, this possibility was not considered by the Joint Committee on Official Languages, when it discussed the 1991 census.

The bluntness of the proposed question is probably unwelcome to Statistics Canada, which seems to have a policy of encouraging multiple responses to census questions on home language, mother tongue, and ethnicity. However, such bluntness seems necessary if the federal and provincial governments are to have the information they need to carry out official-language policies.

Appendix A:
Historical Data

As has been noted in chapter 3, historical census data must be used only with caution. In part, this caution is related to the fact that the census questionnaire has changed over time. However, it must be appreciated that there have also been changes in the wording of questions, in the instructions accompanying the questions, in the editing procedures applied to the answers, and even in the attitude of respondents, affecting the way in which they reply to certain questions (an often-cited example of this last factor is the sharp decline in persons declaring German origin during the periods when Canada was at war with that country).

Acknowledging the existence of these and other factors, which complicate any comparison of data obtained from different censuses, it is still a useful source of information to see a table giving the historical answers to various census questions.

The tables that follow should be read with this cautionary note in mind. Complete comparability cannot be expected but the trends are usually visible and often of value.

TABLE 18

Total population and population of French home language, Canada, censuses of 1971, 1981, and 1986[a]

Census year	Total population	French HL Number	% of total
1971	21,568,315	5,546,025	25.7
1981	24,083,495	5,923,010	24.6
1986	25,022,005	6,015,680[b]	24.0

Sources: 1971, census of Canada; 1981 and 1986, *Adjusted Language Data*
[a] The 'home language' question was asked of only a sample of the population, which excluded 'inmates of institutions,' in 1981 and 1986; the total populations shown for those years are lower than in table 19, which had no exclusions.
[b] In 1986, after imputations, the single response 'French' was reported for only 5,798,470 persons (23.2 per cent of the total population); the additional 217,210 in this table represents allocation of multiple responses.

TABLE 19

Total population and population of French mother tongue, Canada, censuses of 1931 to 1986

Census year	Total population	French MT Number	% of total
1931[a]	10,376,786	2,832,298	27.3
1941[a]	11,506,655	3,354,753	29.2
1951	14,009,429	4,068,850	29.0
1961	18,238,247	5,123,151	28.1
1971	21,568,315	5,793,650	26.9
1976	22,992,605	5,966,707	25.9
1981	24,343,180	6,249,095	25.7
1986	25,309,340	6,354,840[b]	25.1

Sources: 1971 and earlier are from the census of Canada; 1976 figures are as calculated by Linda Demers and John Kralt in *On the Comparability of Mother Tongue Data, 1976–1981* (Ottawa: Statistics Canada 1983); and 1981 and 1986 figures are from *Adjusted Language Data.*
[a] Data for Newfoundland are not included in 1931 and 1941. In 1931, the census question was different from that asked at subsequent censuses, but the data are probably reasonably comparable.
[b] In 1986, after imputations, the single response 'French' was reported for only 6,159,740 persons (24.3 per cent of the total population); the additional 195,100 in this table represents allocation of multiple responses.

TABLE 20
Total population and population of French origin, Canada, censuses of 1881 to 1971

Census year	Total population	French origin	
		Number	% of total
1881[a]	4,324,810	1,298,929	30.0
1901	5,371,315	1,649,371	30.7
1911	7,204,838	2,061,719	28.6
1921	8,788,483	2,452,743	27.9
1931	10,376,786	2,927,990	28.2
1941	11,506,655	3,483,038	30.3
1951[b]	14,009,429	4,319,167	30.8
1961	18,238,247	5,540,346	30.4
1971[c]	21,568,310	6,180,120	28.7

[a] The question on origin was not asked in 1891.
[b] Data for Newfoundland not included prior to 1951.
[c] Until 1971, a person's ethnic origin was (generally) traced through the paternal line. In 1981, the question was materially changed, to allow respondents to trace their origin through the maternal line. For this reason, 1971 has been used as the cut-off data of this table.

Note that home language and mother tongue may be different from ethnic origin (and from each other).

TABLE 21
Official bilingualism in each of several areas of Canada, censuses of 1961 to 1986

Census year	Area	Total population	Bilinguals[a]	
			Number	% of total
1961	CANADA	18,238[b]	2,231	12.2
	Quebec	5,259	1,339	25.5
	NB	598	113	19.0
	Ontario	6,236	493	7.9
	Elsewhere	6,145	286	4.6
1971	CANADA	21,568	2,900	13.4
	Quebec	6,028	1,664	27.6
	NB	635	136	21.5
	Ontario	7,703	716	9.3
	Elsewhere	7,203	384	5.3
1981	CANADA	24,083	3,682	15.3
	Quebec	6,369	2,065	32.4
	NB	689	183	26.5
	Ontario	8,534	924	10.8
	Elsewhere	8,491	510	6.0

TABLE 21 (*continued*)

Census year	Area	Total population	Bilinguals[a] Number	Bilinguals[a] % of total
1986	CANADA	25,022	4,056	16.2
	Quebec	6,454	2,227	34.5
	NB	702	204	29.1
	Ontario	9,001	1,058	11.7
	Elsewhere	8,864	568	6.4

[a] 'Bilinguals' are those who claimed to be able to carry on a conversation in English and French.
[b] All numbers are in thousands.

TABLE 22
Total population and immigrant population, Canada, censuses of 1881 to 1986

Census year	Total population	Immigrants Number	Immigrants % of total
1881	4,325[a]	609	14.1
1901	5,371	700	13.0
1911	7,205	1,587	22.0
1921	8,788	1,956	22.3
1931	10,377	2,308	22.2
1941	11,507	2,019	17.5
1951[b]	14,009	2,060	14.7
1961	18,238	2,844	15.6
1971[c]	21,568	3,296	15.3
1981	24,083	3,843	16.0
1986	25,022	3,908	15.6

[a] All numbers are in thousands.
[b] Data for Newfoundland not included prior to 1951. Also, prior to 1951, persons born in Newfoundland were counted as being immigrants to Canada.
[c] Until 1971 (inclusive), all persons born outside Canada were counted. In 1981 and 1986, the count excluded persons born abroad but who were Canadian citizens by birth.

Appendix B:
Language Data of the
1986 Census

The most recent census of Canada was taken on 4 June 1991, but the results were not available at the time this book went to press. Data reported by the 1986 census, presented in this appendix, are the most up-to-date available.

As noted in chapter 3, there were three questions on language asked in 1986. 'Mother tongue' was asked of all persons; the other two, 'home language' and 'official languages spoken,' appeared only on the long-form questionnaire sent to a one-fifth sample of the non-institutional population.

The five pairs of tables that follow present the responses received to the 'mother tongue' and 'home language' questions for Canada as a whole, Quebec, Ontario, New Brunswick, and Canada exclusive of these three provinces. All are from Statistics Canada publications; the upper table of each pair shows the populations of each of the three major language groups, as these are usually quoted; the lower table shows the actual answers to the census questions, the only editing being the imputation of languages to those respondents who did not reply to one or both of these two questions. The numbers in the upper tables were derived from those of the lower tables by applying factors calculated from the 1981 (not 1986) data, for distribution of the various multiple responses.

The upper table of each pair is taken from *Adjusted Language Data*, published by Statistics Canada in April 1988; the lower table is taken from Statistics Canada 1986 census publications *Language: Part 1*, Catalogue no. 93-102 (mother tongue) (Ottawa 1987) and *Language: Part 2*, Catalogue no. 93-103 (home language) (Ottawa 1989).

The following information applies to all tables in Appendix B:

- The abbreviation 'MT' means 'by mother tongue'; this is defined as being the first language (or languages) learned in childhood and still understood, even if no longer spoken.
- 'HL' means 'by home language,' the language (or languages) now spoken by the respondent when in his or her own home, regardless of the language(s) spoken by that person at work or elsewhere.
- The 'mother tongue' question was asked of all persons, so the total shown under each MT column reflects the full population count. However, the HL totals are just over 1 per cent lower, chiefly reflecting the deliberate exclusion of 'inmates of institutions' from the sample to which the 2B (long-form) questionnaires had been sent.
- In each of the lower tables, 'SR' means that the single response 'English' or 'French' was given to the question.
- The line 'Non-official' includes both single and multiple responses that did not mention either English or French and therefore includes all languages except English and French.

TABLE 23
Adjusted language data for Canada, by mother tongue and by home language, 1986

Language	MT	HL
English	15,709,650 (62.1%)	17,249,900 (68.9%)
French	6,354,840 (25.1%)	6,015,680 (24.0%)
Non-official	3,244,850 (12.8%)	1,756,425 (7.0%)

TABLE 24
Unadjusted census data for Canada, by mother tongue and by home language, 1986

Language	MT	HL
English (SR)	15,334,085	16,595,535
French (SR)	6,159,740	5,798,470
Non-official	2,874,285	1,475,835
English + French	332,610	351,900
English + non-official	525,720	712,445
French + non-official	36,310	40,055
English + French + non-official	46,585	47,755
Total	25,309,330	25,022,005

TABLE 25
Adjusted language data for Quebec, by mother tongue and by home language, 1986

Language	MT	HL
English	678,785 (10.4%)	796,695 (12.3%)
French	5,408,980 (82.8%)	5,343,210 (82.8%)
Non-official	444,695 (6.8%)	314,600 (4.9%)

TABLE 26
Unadjusted census data for Quebec, by mother tongue and by home language, 1986

Language	MT	HL
English (SR)	580,030	676,050
French (SR)	5,316,925	5,223,370
Non-official	394,910	276,095
English + French	150,730	164,580
English + non-official	29,875	45,170
French + non-official	30,635	37,860
English + French + non-official	29,350	31,355
Total	6,532,465	6,454,490

TABLE 27
Adjusted language data for New Brunswick, by mother tongue and by home language,
1986

Language	MT	HL
English	462,935 (65.3%)	478,125 (68.1%)
French	237,570 (33.5%)	219,350 (31.3%)
Non-official	8,940 (1.3%)	4,385 (0.6%)

TABLE 28
Unadjusted census data for New Brunswick, by mother tongue and by home language,
1986

Language	MT	HL
English (SR)	450,970	464,985
French (SR)	225,590	208,545
Non-official	7,910	3,590
English + French	23,050	22,355
English + non-official	1,650	2,130
French + non-official	75	20
English + French + non-official	200	230
Total	709,440	701,855

TABLE 29
Adjusted language data for Ontario, by mother tongue and by home language, 1986

Language	MT	HL
English	7,097,920 (78.0%)	7,798,355 (86.6%)
French	484,265 (5.3%)	340,545 (3.8%)
Non-official	1,519,505 (16.7%)	862,270 (9.6%)

TABLE 30
Unadjusted census data for Ontario, by mother tongue and by home language, 1986

Language	MT	HL
English (SR)	6,941,930	7,492,440
French (SR)	424,720	281,615
Non-official	1,361,405	727,095
English + French	104,550	111,320
English + non-official	254,525	375,965
French + non-official	3,540	1,750
English + French + non-official	11,015	10,995
Total	9,101,690	9,001,165

TABLE 31
Adjusted language data for elsewhere in Canada, by mother tongue and by home language, 1986

Language	MT	HL
English	7,470,010 (83.3%)	8,176,720 (92.2%)
French	224,025 (2.5%)	112,575 (1.3%)
Non-official	1,271,710 (14.2%)	575,165 (6.5%)

TABLE 32
Unadjusted census data for elsewhere in Canada, by mother tongue and by home language, 1986

Language	MT	HL
English (SR)	7,361,155	7,962,060
French (SR)	192,505	84,940
Non-official	1,110,060	469,055
English + French	54,280	53,645
English + non-official	239,670	289,180
French + non-official	2,060	425
English + French + non-official	6,020	5,175
Total	8,965,725	8,864,495

Index